TABLE OF CONTENTS

CHAPTER III

## Abstract

There has been a significant amount of research based on familes and their dynamics. Much of todays reseach focuses on the effects of parental absence. This study adresses the specific phenomenon of paternal abscece in a males life; however, the inquiry is focused on the child's perception of the absence and the role such understanding plays in their lives. This study will require 9 male participants. The study required examining indivdual's ideas and understandings of their father which was done in a qualitative manner. This study adresses an indivduals thoughts and feelings regarding their father rather than quantitatively examining a larger poulation of fatherless males. This study adresses how such percetions were developed and how they currently manifest. This study also attepmts to focus on indivdual understandings of their fathers abscence. The questions to be addressed are; how does a child's *positive*, *negative*, or *neutral* perception of an absent father develop, and is such perception relevant to the manner or reason for their father's absence? The findings included an emphasis on the importance of perception rather than situation. It also suggests clinical implications for individuals who were raised without a father such as; exploring their feelings/perception of their father, working on changing faulty perceptions, and identifying defenses that are used to cope.

## Perceptions of Fatherlessness

Single-parent families have been under scrutiny and research for the past few decades. May researchers present the view that two-parent families provide a healthier stepping stone for child's development when compared to a single-parent or blended family (Pleck, 1997). In other words, much research suggests that society holds traditional two-parent families as providing the ideal environment for child development (Krieder, 2005).

### Family Blends and the Father's Role

Recent research focuses on different family structures, because an increasing number of children are raised in single-parent homes, particularly in father-absent homes (Krieder & Fields, 2005). Over twenty-five million American children (or 33.5 percent of children in the U.S.) live without biological fathers (Krieder & Fields, 2005), even as, the father's role has been magnified, and thought of as an extremely important aspect of a child's development. Indeed, recent literature notes the importance of the father's role and how it can have both positive and negative impacts on children (Updegraff, McHale, Crouter, & Kupanoff, 2001). Typically the father's role is to provide financial support, act as a disciplinarian, protect the child, and model the masculinity. However, research has shown negative effects of paternal presence as the father can be abusive, neglectful, and impose detrimental emotions and behaviors into their children.

### Reasons for Absent Fathers

Fatherlessness can be an outcome of many circumstances; for example, there are increasing numbers of children being raised with no father because of the increases in divorce, war, imprisonment, in out-of-wedlock births, and in the number of lesbian and single women having children through artificial insemination. These distinctive situations may lead to different outcomes and may have varying effects on children. In other words, there may be differences in children who lost a father due to war compared to those who lost a father because imprisonment or divorce. For example, in the past decade, research found that children born by the use of donor insemination and raised by two lesbian mothers were well adjusted, both emotionally and behaviorally, and that family dynamics in lesbian mother families is similar to that of heterosexual families (Brewaeys, Ponjaert, Van Hall, & Golombok, 1997). These findings suggest that, as long as children have good enough, loving parents, they are more likely to be well- adjusted.

**Effects of Fatherlessness**

Based on the view regarding how essential a father is to a child's life, one might wonder what it is about a father's absence that leads to poorer childhood outcomes. Several theories have been put forth, the three most popular are economic deprivation, poor parenting, and lack of social support (Lamb, 2004), although they are not the only ones.

Most research results indicate numerous undesirable outcomes for children who are raised apart from their biological father (Lamb, 2004); for example in heterosexual families, fatherlessness has been reported to lead to more emotional disturbances, school dropouts, drug addiction, earlier sexual behavior, academic difficulties, lower self-esteem, and an increased risk of incarceration (Horn, 2002). Specifically, results from over 30 years of research indicate that a father's absence negatively affects children in a multitude of ways that primarily fit into the following 3 categories: (1) Academic performance (e.g., under-achievement, truancy); (2) Psychological problems (e.g., low self-esteem, depression, anxiety); and (3) Behavioral difficulties (e.g., disobedience; alcohol & drug use, promiscuity) (Horn, 2002).

When examining fatherlessness within heterosexual families/couples, three dominant explanations exist for why a father's absence adversely affects children's lives (Lamb, 2004).

First, parental absence is seen as having only one parent in the household, ultimately leading to a less congenial environment for socializing children effectively. Furthermore, economic disadvantage and family conflict have been known to impact a child's development. More specifically, family conflict in this situation can best be described as problems and issues arising out of divorce or separation (Lamb, 2004).

The effects of divorce and single parenthood have been one focus of attention in studies looking at the negative influences on child development (e.g., lack of emotional support, lack of structure, and parental discord). Most of the studies look beyond the children for causes (e.g., tumultuous divorce, economic factors, and lack of a role model); however, because most of these factors cannot be controlled, it could be beneficial to identify mitigating factors that might help single parents and counselors understand such negative effects on children.

**Research Discrepancies Surrounding Fatherlessness**

Discrepancies exist among research results regarding the correlations between fatherlessness and risk of children's poor academic performance, psychological problems, or behavioral difficulties, because some children from fatherless homes thrive. For example, children who grew up with lesbian mothers did not experience all the negative outcomes suggested some research on to children who grow up without a father (Brewaeys et al., 1997). Arguably, other factors come into play, such as the type of household and support experienced by a child. Unfortunately, there is limited research on children of lesbian mothers/homosexual fathers, and adjustment is unknown.

Furthermore, other research supports the idea that fatherlessness, as related to the biological father, is not the main reason for negative outcomes in children. A review of literature looking at the three dominant explanations found only limited support that marital conflict is associated with negative outcomes (Brewaeys et al., 1997). Interestingly enough, research on adopted children show similar outcomes that are seen in fatherless children (e.g., low self-esteem, behavioral problems, drug use, and increased promiscuity). The negative interaction between parental figures affects the child similar to that of a child whose father is completely absent.

One possible reason for the lack of consistency in research findings is it's inattention to a child's perception of his/her absent father and how it related to their own functioning (e.g., emotional well-being, academic performance, self-esteem). This seems to be important because of findings that socio-genealogical connectedness leads to the general well-being of children (Medinnus, 1965). For instance, research results have demonstrated that parental separation as a result of incarceration, was associated with problematic child behavior when knowledge of one's parental whereabouts was disclosed (Fritsch & Burkhead, 1981). Yet, the study found no significant relationship among children who believed their absent parent was away at school, working, in the hospital, staying with relatives, or absent for other socially acceptable reasons. Accordingly, this study demonstrated that it was not the father's absence, per se, that correlated with problematic behavior in children, but, rather, the combination of the father's absence and the knowledge that they were absent due to imprisonment (Fritsch & Burkhead, 1981). Mediating factors such as environment and financial stability had significant influences on the child; however, the fathers absence and the child's understanding of their father were considerably strong variables.

Moreover, one study looking at the differences between delinquent and non-delinquent children found that there were significantly marked differences between those children's perceptions of their fathers (Medinnus, 1965). Despite these two findings, which date far back, little research has been done to understand the child's perceptions of his/her father and its developmental course. What are the components of a child's perception? How does a child's perception develop? What key factors play a role in a child's opinion of his or her absent father.

## Self-Influence

Many studies focused on the father's role have failed to acknowledge the child's influence on their own outcome (e.g., emotional well-being, self-esteem, conduct issues). Popenoe (2000) explained there was a time in the past when fatherlessness was far more common than it is today, but death was to blame, not divorce, desertion and out of wedlock births. Almost all of today's fatherless children have fathers who are alive and perfectly capable of shouldering the responsibilities of fatherhood. Children whose father's had died did not show the same outcomes of those whose father's were still alive. Children today are simply loosing parents in a different way than before, with significantly different outcomes. The "Fragile Families" study showed that 81% of unmarried fathers are either cohabitating or romantically involved with their child's mother at birth. By the time the child is five, most couples broke up and the father's involvement has steadily declined. In a study of 5000 participants, 40% of fathers have no or little contact with their children. (McLanahan, Garfinkel, Reichman, Teitler, Carlson, & Audigier, 2003).

## Negative Outcomes

There are many negative outcomes that have been found to correlate with the absence of fathers. Popenoe (2000) showed juvenile violent crime had increased six fold from 16,000 arrests in 1960 to 96,000 in 1992. Eating disorders and rates of depression have soared among adolescent girls. He also explained 60% of America's rapist, 72% of adolescent murders, and 70% of long term prison inmates came from fatherless homes.

Alongside, Hymowitz (2007) suggested children of fatherless homes are more likely to suffer emotional, behavior, and psychological problems and children from fatherless homes are five times more likely to suffer from poverty. He showed the risk of neglect doubles, and the probability of accidents and injuries triples. There is also an increased risk of developing antisocial behaviors, engaging in premarital sex, and substance abuse (Hyrowitz, 2007).

Popenoe's (2000) research also suggested that it is decidedly worse for a child to lose a father in the modern voluntary way than through death. The child had a rational for his father's absence, now the ambiguity of an absent father has more emotional factors that are salient in his or her life. Much of the current research suggests children of divorced and never married mothers, are still successful in life, even though they have had no contact with a biological father (Popenoe, 2000). The question is the type of absence a child perceives. Does the type of absence play a role in the child's outcome?

**Parental Alienation**

There has been a new phrase created in the body of research regarding children's perceptions of their father's absence, "parental alienation." This is the attempt by one parent to turn the child's affection from the other parent by reciting the darkest flaws, imagined, exaggerated, or real of the other parent. This type of practice significantly skews the child's perception of his or her absent parent (Hymowitz 2007). Furthermore, this study attempts to understand perceptions of a father's absence and how it has been developed

Research supports child-father relationships because it has been shown to have major effects on children (Lamb, 2004). It is important to continue research in order to strengthen our understanding for our next generations, which is continuing the trend of single parent homes. A more sound understanding of fatherlessness influences, may aid in the betterment of society.

**Statement of the Problem**

Looking at the significant role a father fulfills has been a major focus for social scientist in the past 30 years. Researchers have come to understand the importance of a father in their child's emotional, psychological, financial, and educational well-being. The trend of fatherless homes has increased, and researchers are starting to take different approaches in terms of children's outcomes. Popenoe (2000) explains, in the past three decades, between 1960 and 1990, the percentage of children living apart from their biological fathers more than doubled, from 17% to 36%. Popenoe (2002) also suggested, 50% of children in the United States go to sleep each evening without being able to say good night to their biological fathers. Another researcher suggests over twenty-five million American children (or 33.5 percent of children in the U.S.) live absent their biological father (Krieder, 2005). However the data is classified or labeled, the fact is there is an enormous amount of children living without their fathers.

Delving further in the background of children and their fathers, a 1981 survey of children who were living apart from their fathers found that 52% of children had not seen them at all in more than a year; only 16% saw their fathers as often as once a week (Popenoe 2000). Many reasons have come up for the increase in fatherless homes; these fathers may be in jail, the military, away at work, never present at all, divorced without custody or visitation, sperm donors, or any other possible combination of other priorities. Social scientists discussed the decline in fatherhood as being a major force behind most of the problems with America's youth: crime, premature sexuality, out of wedlock births in adolescents, depression, substance abuse, decreasing educational achievement, and the growing number of children in poverty (Popenoe, 2000).

## Purpose of the Study

Most of the research today looks at socioeconomic factors associated with a father's absence. They concluded that children who grow up in father-absent homes are five times more likely to be poor, suggesting fatherlessness causes adolescent poverty. They looked at the absence of the father's role in the child's outcome rather than looking at the child's own processing in relation to their development. The majority of literature points to a statistical correlation between the father's absence and childhood outcomes. They look at the father's involvement as it relates legal trouble, mental health problems, educational attainment, and financial stability. Research suggests a strong implication of correlation; since father absence is associated with poorer outcomes for children. Current research does not then suggests that father absence is, in and of itself, is the cause of negative outcomes as it's so widely perceived? There are other factors that this study will attempt to identify as it is related

This study will supplement the literature by addressing the issue of father absence, though from the perspective of selected participants and their perceptions. It is important to understand the way a individual perceives his/her absent father. Some variables are external and beyond a individual's control (e.g., reasons a father is not in the home, maternal influence on the child's understanding of his or her absent father, sibling perceptions of the absent father, and lack of role models). This research will study internal cognitive and emotional processes in relation to an individual's environment rather than solely placing responsibility on external factors. This research is searching for ways a child or an adult can adapt to a fatherless home, instead of further proving why absence can be detrimental.

Psychologist Louise Silverstien and Carl Auerbach argued, "It is not fathers, but the stability of the emotional connection and predictability of the caretaking relationship that are significant variables which predict positive outcomes" (p. 397, 1999). The purpose of this study is to investigate an individual's perception of his or her absent father and how it has developed. How does a individual's positive, negative, or neutral perception of an absent father develop, and is such perception relevant to the manner or reason for their father's absence? In this study it will also be important to address cognitive and emotional factors that have been components of an individual's perception of their absent father. This study will also present treatment implications for individuals who were raised without their fathers; especially focused on their perceived experience. The overall purpose of this study is to examine the experiences of adults who grew up in fatherless homes.

# CHAPTER II

## Literature Review

If, prior to the 70's, individuals were to be asked about the role his or her father's presence or absence had on their well-being, they would have found themselves struggling to find research with the answer. This is due to the type of research done on families. If today, that same someone were to ask that question, he or she would still find themselves struggling, but this time it would be a matter of interpreting the research. This is because currently, there are volumes of available research on the effects of a father's presence or absence. Increases in war, divorce, incarceration, and importance of family research have identified changes in family structure and dynamics in relation to absence of a father. However, due to the several different ways in which "absence" and "presence" have been defined, even in its simplest form, the conclusive evidence of the role the father has in his child's development is inconclusive or at the very least, confusing. For example, in one study, Way and Stauber (1996) interviewed 45 adolescent girls about their relationships with their fathers. Of the 26 girls who did not live with their fathers and who can be interpreted as having an absent father, seven reported weekly contact with them; 10 reported occasional contact; while only nine reported almost no contact. For the purpose of this research, father absence will be defined as a child growing up in a home where he has not had face to face contact with his father for at least 5 years.

The most frequently mentioned cause of paternal absence occurs when a father is away is due to career demands, or divorced from the child's mother. For those children who are dealing with a temporary loss, such as one due to career relocation, fewer negative effects have been attributed to father-absence (Blankenhorn, 1995; Horn, 2002). However, in the case of divorce or death, a more serious impact has been found on the child's development (Horn, 2002). Another aspect making interpretation challenging, are the reports by researchers concluding that there is a differential effect of age on the severity of impact of father absence (see Biller, 1993 & Biller & Meredith, 1997). These differences in effects may be due to the inferior coping mechanisms of children compared with the more advanced skills of adolescence, who have achieved increased emotional maturity and access to supportive social networks in the form of peer groups (Steinberg, 1989). As Beaty (1995) reports, children who become father absent before the age of five suffer more debilitating intra-psychological interpersonal difficulties than do children who become father absent after the age of five. Thus, for children who have never had contact with their father, the effects seem to be more profound and long-term.

Due to a lack of cohesiveness on how children were studied in relations to their fathers, this paper will breakdown the information available and describe the role of a father's presence or absence in its most basic form. What it's most basic form means is that father's presence will be operationally defined as, the biological father living under the same roof as his son or daughter from birth. Father's absence will be operationally defined as, the biological father being absent from their child's life for at least three years during their childhood or adolescence.

The purpose of this literature review is to understand and explore the research on paternal absence as it relates to sons and daughters. This will be done by using the most simplistic descriptions for presence and absence and to discuss the limitations that have led research to shift away from such an explicit look at this topic. The following five questions are addressed: (1) what types of research have been reported on a father's role in his child's development over the last four decades? (2) What types of literature were reviewed for study? (3) What predictions can be made about sons simply based on the presence or absence of their father? (4) What predictions can be made about daughters simply based on the presence or absence of their father? (5) What limitations have prevented researchers from such a straightforward look at a father's role in his sons or daughters development? Following will be a brief discussion interpreting the literature; methodological issues will be addressed, as well as implications for future research.

## Theoretical Conceptualization

### Attachment Theory

Attachment theory provides a descriptive and explanatory framework for discussion of affectionate relationships between human beings; particularly caregivers. The theory was firstly developed by John Bowlby in 1969, and has remained an influential framework, which is still widely used to explain many childhood outcomes including mental health outcomes and interpersonal relationship outcomes (Hazan, & Shaver, 1987). Bowlby's work was enhanced by Harry Harlow, who discovered infant monkeys separated from their mothers would cling to fluffy covered objects rather than wire-coated food dispensers. Results concluded by stating the importance of an infant's need for nurturing as part of a secure attachment (Harlow & Suomi, 1970). Attachment theory, thus, offers that individual's attachment style is influenced by the relationship between a child and his or her primary care givers and that the attachment style remains durable into adulthood (Bowlby, 1969).

Bowlby (1973) also discussed the notion of internal working models, which are essentially mental representations that children form about their relationship experiences with their attachment-figures. These representations formulate the child's belief system about the social world. In a similar regard, Schneider (1991) has suggested that individuals carry with them cognitive representations of their attachment figures and their experiences with them. There is a wide-held notion among developmental theorists that a child who fails to experience positive cognitive representations of their attachment relationships will be susceptible to emotional, behavioral, and relationships problems. Negative attachment experiences, such as inconsistency or disruption in the parent-child relationship, parent-child separations, threats of abandonment, and/or abandonment are thought to increase such susceptibility (Holmes, 1993).

Children raised in the type of environment that Holmes describes are said to have insecurely attached personality styles (1993). Hence, according to attachment theory, the increasing societal trend of children being raised in single-parent homes increases children's risk for developing insecure attachment styles. With regard to the marked increase in single-parent families, a complementary developmental approach to attachment theory seems wise to adopt.

**Cognitive-Developmental**

A cognitive-developmental perspective that focuses on a child's perceived reality proposes that humans are innately wired to desire an understanding of their relationships. Furthermore there exists a need for a sense of genealogical connectedness. Socio-genealogical connectedness refers to the extent to which children identify with their natural parents' biological and social backgrounds. This identification is rooted in the amount of knowledge and the quality of that knowledge. Where a child knows a lot of quality information about their parents, there exists a positive correlation to that child's identification with his or her parents. Thus, the quantitatively less and/or the more damaging the information is, the less likely it is that the child will identify with the parent the information is associated with.

Previous research that demonstrates the importance of genealogical connectedness has looked at adopted children who often have similar kinds of problems that are seen with children reared without their father. Such problems include aggression, stealing, lying, rebelliousness, truancy, low self-esteem, depression, illicit drug use, promiscuity, and academic difficulties

(Brodzinsky, 1990). According to Brodzinsky these issues develop as a direct result of genealogical loss experienced by the adopted children (1987).

Consequently, children raised without their father could have some knowledge, no knowledge, or be uncertain and/or confused about their father. This will lead to these children perceiving their father as positive, negative, or neutral. Any one of these conditions has the potential to strengthen or undermine a child's perceived attachment and thus affecting their mental health, academic and relationship outcomes later in life.

**Rational Emotive Behavior Therapy (REBT)**

Further research involving perceptions and their influence on behavior is seen in Albert Ellis's *Rational Emotive Behavior Therapy* (REBT). According to Ellis (1995), REBT is based on the premise that whenever we become upset, it is not the events taking place in our lives that upset us; it is the beliefs that we hold that cause us to become depressed, anxious, enraged, etc. Ellis derived his theory from Epictetus, a philosopher who lived in ancient Greece from AD 55-AD 135. Epictetus stated, "Men are disturbed not by events, but by the views which they take of them" (Ellis, 1995).

Ellis (1995) explains rational emotive behavior therapy emphasizes the belief that emotionally healthy human beings develop an acceptance of reality, even when reality is highly unpleasant. There are three types of acceptance: (1) unconditional self-acceptance; (2) unconditional other-acceptance; and (3) unconditional life-acceptance. Each of these types of acceptance is based on three core beliefs:

(1) *Unconditional self-acceptance*:

I am a fallible human being; I have my good points and my bad points; there is no reason why I must not have flaws. Despite my good points and my bad points, I am no more worthy and no less worthy than any other human being.

(2) *Unconditional other-acceptance*:

Other people will treat me unfairly from time to time. There is no reason why they must treat me fairly. The people who treat me unfairly are no more worthy and no less worthy than any other human being.

(3) *Unconditional life-acceptance*:

Life doesn't always work out the way that I'd like it to. There is no reason why life must go the way I want it to. Life is not necessarily pleasant but it is never awful and it is nearly always bearable.

Ellis's rational emotive behavior therapy theorizes that our reaction to having our goals blocked (or even the possibility of having them blocked) is determined by our beliefs (Ellis, 1995). The utilization of an ABC model of behavior beliefs and their consequences shows how beliefs of the environment cause emotional and behavioral responses. In the ABC model, something happens (A; action), a belief is created about the situation (B; belief), an emotional and/or behavioral reaction is directly tied to the belief (C; consequence). An individual's belief about their absent father can potentially affect to how they feel towards him, consequently their behavioral and emotional reactions are products of their perceptions and beliefs. Behavioral and emotional reactions have less to do with the father's absence and are more relevant to an individual's belief of their father.

The ABC model shows that A (action) does not cause C (consequence). It is B (belief) that causes C (consequence). When a child grows up in a fatherless home, the results of their actions and internal experiences are not a product of an absent paternal figure. Instead, their beliefs of their absent father as well as implications of fatherlessness are more relevant to the individuals feelings and behaviors.

**Research and Findings on the Father's Role**

Today more American children are growing up without their biological father in the home than at any other point in American history. There have been trends such as divorce and children being born outside of marriage result in a diminishing role of fathers that have increased.

Father absence was of interest to only a limited amount of social scientists prior to the later 20th century; however, it became the focus of considerable research, theory, and speculation over the last four decades. As a result, a large body of literature has accumulated, and substantial advances have been made in efforts to understand father-child relationships, paternal influences on child development, and the particular impact of father involvement on children and families (see Lamb, 2004, for a detailed review). Over the course of the 20th century and beyond, however, the ways in which fatherhood has been operationalized varies considerably, making it difficult to gather conclusive evidence. Perhaps, this rapid shifting is related more to societal attitude changes such as feminism, rather than by social scientist and mental health researchers. More likely it has been a manifestation of both.

The dominant principal guiding research on fatherhood has gone from an emphasis on moral guidance, to breadwinning, to sex-role modeling, marital support, and finally, nurturance (Pleck and Pleck, 1997). Corresponding with these changing disciplines was a shift from a focus on qualitative dimensions of fatherhood such as, masculinity and dominance to quantifiable dimensions, such as the amount of time spent by fathers with their children. Moreover, with the facilitation of the less regarded correlation and/or uncomplicated studies that will be the basis of this review, more detailed and evolved controlled studies had a basis to be carried out.

**Effects of Paternal Absence on the Brain**

Little research has been conducted to identify biological implications on a child's brain due to an absent father. However, neurologists are now finding that growing up without a father actually changes the brain. Braun's (2006) study focused on degus rodents, who are generally raised by both mother and father, in an attempt to understand the effects of paternal absence on the brain. In the study, Braun (2006) raised eight pups (half raised with a father and mother and half raised only with their mother) where the father was removed one day after birth. Wilson (1982) has conducted significant research on these animals and explains that "male degus invest enormous efforts in the upbringing of their young." While maternal contact decreases over time, paternal contact increases as their offspring age (Wilson 1982). Much like humans, the father serves as a source of multiple sensory and emotional aspects of healthy psychosocial and neurological development.

After twenty-one days the degus offspring were examined and differences were found in brain anatomy and behaviors of the rodents. The researchers utilized three techniques to investigate the neural anatomy of the degus offspring; light microscopy, electron microscopy, and weighing the brain. Neurons were examined using an Olympus BH-2 microscope with a final magnification of X1000. The results found differences in the dendrites between groups. Dendrites, which conduct and receive electrical signals other nerves in the body, have a structure called dendritic spines which are responsible for contact between other neurons. Braun (2006) found at twenty-one days of paternal absence, the fatherless group had less dense dendritic spines compared to animals raised by both parents, however these dendritic connections caught up to the opposing group after ninety days.

There were also neural difference found in the amygdala, which is related to emotional response and fear. There were also differences in the orbitofrontal cortex (OFC) which is responsible for decision making. Compared to pups raised by both mother and father, the paternal deprived group had fewer dendritic spines in the OFC and exhibit enlarged dendritic connections in the amygdala (Braun, 2006).

The paternally deprived degus offspring also exhibited behavior differences compared to the opposite group. These rodents showed more aggressive and impulsive behaviors. Researchers observed this in their play, as they engaged in fighting behaviors and aggressive interactions. They also exhibited more anxious behavior and less spending time or engaging with novel rodents who were place in their cage (Braun, 2006).

Although this information gives significant insight into the dynamics of family and its effects on the brain, study's like this should not be directly associated with human beings. The results should be understood carefully as the human brain differs from the rodents in especially in the OFC where decisions are made. The social interactions and interpersonal phenomena differ in incredible ways across various aspects. However, it should be noted that paternal absence has an influence on an offspring's brain and behavior. To conclude specific structures of a human's brain might be misleading and prove to be untrue.

The importance of the father has been emphasized across various disciplines, through various scopes, with the utilization and construction of multiple theories. The emphasis on paternal importance is increasingly relevant and has begun to evolve for the purpose of scientific investigation. The brain, its structure and function, are the future of research for the phenomena on paternal absence. Through a meta-analysis of research on fatherlessness, one can conclude that the father's role is an important one and their functions serve multiple purposes. The need for a father to be present and provided many forms of stimulation is a key component, accompanied with maternal nurturing, in children's development.

## Development of Psychopathology

In both males and females, the absence of the father in early childhood has been noted as a component in the development of psychopathology; namely schizophrenia. In an analysis on the development of schizophrenia Bateson, Jackson, Haley, Weakland, (1956) theorized family dynamics and situations that provide a fertile environment in which schizophrenia is facilitated.

This research argued for the position of three general family situations of a schizophrenic; "1) A child whose mother becomes anxious and withdraws if the child responds to her as a loving mother. That is, the child's very existence has a special meaning to the mother which arouses her anxiety and hostility when she is in danger of intimate contact with the child. 2) A mother to whom feelings of anxiety and hostility toward the child are not acceptable, and whose way of denying them is to express overt loving behavior to persuade the child to respond to her as a loving mother and to withdraw from him if he does not. "Loving behavior" does not necessarily imply "affection"; it can, for example, be set in a framework of doing the proper thing, instilling "goodness," and the like. 3) The absence of anyone in the family, such as a strong and insightful father, who can intervene in the relationship between the mother and child and support the child in the face of the contradictions involved" (Bateson et al. 1956).

It is not argued that the absence of a father is sole component in the development of psychopathology; however, the role of the father plays a key component within family dynamics. As seen in the Bateson et al. (1956) theoretical framework, a father's presence can act as a buffer between mother and child potentially facilitating alternative internalizations which can be a deterrent from psychopathology.

## Types of Literature Reviewed

In order to interpret the research on father presence and absence, three major types of literatures were reviewed. They consisted of father absence, single parent families, and divorced families. A more narrow discussion of father absence or an emphasis on studies using the term father presence would have limited the range of available research for this review. Findings from largely correlated studies of father absence reflect that the non-residence of biological fathers has differential effects on boys and girls. Therefore, the findings will be broken down by gender, facilitating a discussion of the most prominent predictors of a father's presence or absence on his son distinct from his daughter.

## The Father's Role in his Son's Development

Much of the psychological research involving childhood development is focused on maternal influences. However, research directed at paternal significance gives us a clear understanding of the importance a father's role in a child's development. During the late 1980s and 1990s, much of this literature evolved into a broader, more inclusive paradigm of father specific parenting roles, relations, and involvement (Johnson 1996). The growing diversity of life courses and residency patterns for men and children has fostered a new awareness about father's roles (Gerson 1993; Griswold 1993; Marsigilio 1995a) as well as the realization that a decreasing proportion of young males today live without biological fathers (Bianchi, 1995; Mintz 1998). A generalized paradigm has been projected through much of past and current research regarding fatherhood. This paradigm proposes that father's absence has a distinct correlation in their sons' outcomes.

Fathers' presence or absence can be a factor motivating specific behaviors in a young male's development. Along with these behaviors, the research has also noted some emotional and cognitive differences. Johnson (1996) argues that the father-absence literature in the area of father-child relations arrives at the conclusion that the absence of fathers has a negative effect on young male's development. The negative effects that Johnson mentions have been examined in terms of intellectual functioning, psychosocial development of males in relation to family structure, and functioning. In accordance with this line of research, other studies show father presence extends beyond physical and fiscal boundaries to practical emotional relations with their sons. The father's presence is a rich and complex construction of roles and relationships with their sons (Ishii-Kuntz, 1992; Marino & McCowan, 1976).

Based on decades of research, the father's role in the home is a major component to protective factors and moral development. Fathers' play styles differ from mothers' play styles with infants; fathers use more of their time playing with their infants (Parke 1981), and their play is more vigorous than their mother's (Clarke-Stewart, 1978). Aggressive contact with a father provides male infants with a unique experience that is linked to developmental outcomes in cognitive skills and sociability (Johnson 1996). Before research done by Lamb (1976a, 1977b), the mother was presumed to be the sons only attachments figure; however a series of research over three decades ago determined conditions where infant males prefer fathers over mothers. Males however, chose the available parent under distress, but the mother is preferred when both parents were present. Father's have been proven to play a very different, and important role when compared to their sons' mothers.

A father's presence increases many protective factors in the development of their sons. Family research provides us with a conclusive perspective that sons and daughters living with single mothers experience the consequence of lost income, poor living conditions, including poorer housing (Edelman, 1987) and increased health risk (Angel & Worobey, 1988). This research provides information that shows a father's presence adds factors to the home which supports their son's healthy development. These factors are increased income, protection from outside dangers, and masculine role modeling.

Father's presence may provide a model and techniques of discipline that causes their sons to view them as facilitators of their socialization (Atkinson & Ogston, 1974). This early research suggested males learned masculinity and aggression from the roles their fathers portrayed. However, Broude (1990) suggested that residential fathers reduce aggressive behaviors in boys attenuating the effects of American culture messages valuing hyper masculinity in men. Johnson

(1996) gives evidence that shows literature to be similar in their conclusion of father's absence and its effects on their sons. Lack of contact with fathers appears to have its most dramatic effect on male children than on female children (e.g., Bee, 1974; Hetherington et al. Cox, 1978; Mott, 1994). The main concerns in this research are identity development (Mitchell & Wilson, 1967), school success, and social prowess as essential ingredients the integration into adult American life and fulfillment of the male provider role (Cazenave, 1979). The father's presence is a strong variable correlated to their son's healthy development and socialization.

**Aggressive Behaviors**

Furthermore, much of the literature shows that there is a high expectation that the behavioral consequences of fatherless sons vary from child to child. A constant pattern of explosive and aggressive behaviors has been noted in young males who have grown up without their biological father. Santrock & Wohlford (1979) proposed males who have grown up without fathers display abnormally high rates of aggressive and antisocial behavior. In their controlled study, they showed boys with fathers were able to delay self gratification more than boys who did not have their fathers. This shows aggressive behaviors in young males who lack their father's presence can be explained by the need to have immediate gratification.

Males without fathers have also have been described as more vulnerable, with more aggressive tendencies; these boys have been compared to males of the same age whose fathers are in the home (i.e,. Montare &Bonne, 1980). These males may feel the need to defend themselves against imagined threats due a sense of heightened external awareness, caused by their father's absence. However, Biller's (1982) research found that greater male aggressive behaviors found in boys with non-residential fathers is due to early lack of identification, feminine etiology, and lack of male modeling socialization toward true healthy masculinity. These boys have been socialized through maternal influences. Paternal influences allow males to mediate aggression and refrain from using it as a tool for self-gratification. They lack in paternal socialization. Without the father modeling behavior the son cannot learn to control his internal aggressive urges. These urges appear when the son is faced with real or imagined risk. Confusion between masculinity and excessive aggression are major forces driving the behaviors of children with absent fathers.

**Masculinity and Sex Role Development**

Literature on masculinity and psychosexual development, particularly in male children, is a central arena of the father's absence research. Biller (1968, 1996, 1971, 1974) who was a prominent force in the research of father absence, focused his studies on sex role development, masculinity and aggression among boys. He indicated that boys growing up without a father's presence are less masculine, and he would argue even effeminate, with the likely developmental outcome of homosexuality. In contrast to this argument, there lies a body of research that found insufficient empirical evidence which described males without fathers to have less masculine identities and homosexual behaviors. (Herzog and Sudia 1973). This would deny the correlation between father's absence and later homosexuality in earlier research.

A review of literature on sex role stereotyping and gender identity found evidence of a relationship between father's absence and presence and child sex role development to be inconclusive (Herzog & Sudia 1973). Early research finds a connection between father's absence and feministic traits, but more current studies show no differences between male's sex role development in sons who have fathers and those who do not. Lamb (1996b) concludes that sex role development is more influenced by warmth and closeness in the father-son relationship than by the father's own masculinity. This may be a factor influencing the similarities between sons with and without fathers. Hyper-masculine fathers may facilitate the same effects as absent fathers to their sons. In terms of masculinity, the presence and absence is not as defining as the father's warmth and closeness to his son.

Gender concepts of absent and present fathers did not differ among preschool children from fatherless homes to those whose father were present. Males from single parent homes were not more effeminate, but were less sex typed when it came to choosing toys (Brenes, Eisenburg, and Helmstadter 1985). Boys whose fathers are absent are not necessarily more feminine, but may be more open to acknowledging feminine like qualities in themselves and in their surroundings. This is opposed to males with fathers who strongly identify with only masculine qualities.

**Cognitive Functioning and School Performance**

In accordance to much of the research regarding father's presence and absence, men's psychological care and emotional generosity with their sons appear to have the greatest long term implications for their child's development (Johnson 1996). Lessing, Zargorin, and Nelson (1979) found children in father-absent households had lower IQ, verbal, and performance scores than children in father present households. Boys' academic performance is mostly reported as being insufficient by father's absence. Parent roles or parent like behavior may be more meaningful than male models for male behavior or mere exposure to adult males (Schell &Courtney 1979). Much of Jonhson's (1996) research also shows male deficits in academic performance whose fathers are absent.

However, Johnson's (1996) research shows a recovery period in academic functioning over a period of two years. Although children whose fathers have left the home show a disruption in academic performance, within two years, most of the children return to their normal patterns of performance. Boys however, experience greater disruption, but girls show greater recovery after their father's initial absence (Johnson 1996). Many studies find that father's absence had a negative effect on the male's cognitive functioning, but others found mixed results or no differences between sons whose fathers were present and those whose fathers were absent.

In connection to their cognitive functioning lies emotional well-being. Studies show that the psychological vulnerability of children from absent fathers are more likely to experience emotional disorders such as depression when compared to father-present households (Johnson 1996). Due to their emotional disturbances, these boys find it difficult to function normally. These emotional disturbances can be tied to the other effects the young males have due to their father's absence.

Table 1
*Effects of Father Presence on Son's Functioning*

| Presence of Fathers | Absence of Fathers |
|---|---|
| <ul><li>Less Aggressive behaviors</li><li>Higher school performance</li><li>Strong cognitive functioning</li><li>Less emotional disturbances</li><li>Clearer definitions of masculinity</li><li>No effects on sexual identity or preference</li></ul> | <ul><li>More aggressive behaviors</li><li>Lower school performance</li><li>Deficits in cognitive functioning</li><li>More emotional disturbances</li><li>Unclear definitions of masculinity</li><li>No effects on sexual identity or preference</li></ul> |

**Summary**

The research suggests there are differences between sons with present fathers and sons with absent fathers. There are many confounding variables that influence this type of research like ethnicity, socioeconomic status and reasons for father's absence. The differences in young males with and without fathers are mostly in regards to aggressive and explosive behaviors. Early research suggests that masculinity and sex role development show differences between these two groups, however current research shows little to no differences within these male children. School performance and cognitive functioning have been shown to be varied between sons with and without their fathers. Much of the research done regarding the effects of absent and present fathers on males is quite similar to the research focusing on females. Much like male differences, females show similar variability between groups with fathers and those without a male presence in the home.

**Father-Daughter Relationships**

Father-daughter relationships have recently been a topic of discussion and under scrutiny in the past couple decades. Freud was one of the first to focus on the child-parent relationship where he defined the Oedipus/Electra complex. It has been known that father-daughter relationships have not received as much attention as mother-daughter relationships and father-son relationships. Also, research tends to generally focus on the mothers role as opposed to the fathers because the mothers are seen to be more of the primary caretakers resulting in a more affective position.

Recently, the father role has been magnified and seen as a much more pertinent aspect of a child's development. Literature has shown the importance of the role of the father and how it can have positive and negative impacts on children. The majority of research focuses on the father-son relationship because that bond is more worldly recognized and commonly seen as an essential for the male's future performance rather than the daughter's. Research only supports the idea that the bond is stronger between the son and father. Fathers tend to spend more time with their sons than with their daughters (Lamb, 1997; Updegraff et al, 2001) and fathers tend to talk, share and give more advice to their sons (Hosley & Montemayor, 1997; Shulman & Krenke, 1996). Generally, regardless of the parents' marital status, daughters and fathers do not communicate as comfortably and feel as close to each other emotionally, unlike the mother-daughter bond where their discussions are more personal (Lamb, 1997). The bond between mother and child are seen to grow stronger over time, while fathers and their children do not (Bengston & Roberts, 2002). It is safe to say, in regard to the father-daughter relationship that the both are not getting as much as they could from their relationship and each other.

So much attention is given to the father-son relationship that the impact that fathers have on their daughters has been ignored. The disparity between sons and daughters and how they can be affected by their father's presence or absence continues to be highlighted throughout research. Interestingly, the father-daughter relationship compared with the father-son relationship tends to result in more damage when the parents divorce (Hetherington, 2003; Knox, 2004). It can be said that, fathers are unaware that their active involvement in their daughter's life plays a vital role in her development and well-being. For example, daughters with good relationships with their fathers are less likely to develop eating disorders (Maine, 2004) or child anxiety (Bogels & Phares, 2008). It is essential for fathers to be just as attuned with their relationship with their son's as well as with their daughters because lasting effects can be associated with the role of the father. Looking at a more basic stand point, the absence and presence of the father has great potential of affecting his daughter.

**Personality Development**

Delving further in to the most primitive research regarding the Electra complex (feminine Oedipal complex), father-daughter relationships are seen to be of major importance in order for females to later relate to men and develop healthy personality characteristics. Freud and later Leonard, M. (1966) found that there is major importance of successfully resolving the feminine Oedipal complex in order to defeat consequences of *fixation*. This idea is believed that if a female is to *resolve* this obstacle, she will then be able to establish a relationship with her father without any sexualized feelings. Once this occurs, the daughter then has the ability to create healthier intimate relations with other men in her life. This idea of being able to have a healthy, loving bond with other men can be achieved because the female accepts her "feminine role" relieving her symptoms of guilt and anxiety. It is also thought that proper and adequate fathering is a requirement for the success of this phase of psychosexual development. Therefore, it can be concluded that the only way for a female to resolve this conflict is to have her father as a part of her life and if the father is absent then many emotions and unwanted feelings might stir up. "Without paternal participation the girl may idealize her father and later, as an adolescent, seek to love in a similar way to this ideal or maintain a preoedipal narcissistic attitude, such that in adolescence she may be unable to give love but rather seeks narcissistic gratification in being loved" (Leonard, M. 32). Although this theory goes back to 1966, later research builds upon this idea and supports it in that women may develop personality flaws.

The presence of the father has great impact on the daughters' emotional, social, and intellectual development (Biller & Weiss, 1970). The presence of the father is important in the daughters overall well-being. When females grow-up in a household without a father, there is higher risk that she will develop a lower sense of self. Self-esteem has been associated to the absence of fathers (Paterson, Pryor, & Field, 1995). Self-esteem has also been linked to depression and eating disorders. Other research found that females who grew up in absent father households as opposed to fathers being present in the household were more likely to have an eating disorder (Botta & Dumlao, 2002). Daughter's show threatening consequences due to the absence of fathers. Overall, females are happier and healthier when growing up in a household with their fathers.

**Sex and Intimacy - Female**

Hetherington (1972), a renowned researcher on father-daughter relationships, emphasized that there is more promiscuous attitudes of girls in father-absent households and more difficulties of these girls forming or maintaining romantic relationships later on in adulthood. Daughters with present fathers tend to have more successful intimate relationships (Amato, 1994). Other studies found the formation of romantic relations to be more difficult for adolescent or adult women from father-absent households. Father absence is shown to play a powerful and overriding risk factor for early onset sexual activity and subsequent teen pregnancy. Father presence provided a major protective effect against these behaviors, even when other risk factors were present (Ellis, et al., 2003).

Other consequences that females may experience growing up in an absent-father home are the development of inappropriate sex role attitudes (Biller & Weiss, 1970). Other research showed that consequences may be seen through promiscuity and interpersonal problems with significant others (Hetherington, 1972; Wallerstein & Kelly, 1976), permissive attitudes and behaviors, and dependency toward males (Hetherington, 1972). In Eberhardt & Schill's (1984) study, results indicated that there may be room to see greater approval seeking from the females. When a father is present in a daughter's life, there is higher likeliness that she will develop more responsible sexual behaviors and decreased risk of sexual behaviors (Quinlan, 2003).

Taking a more scientific stance, there has been postulations and some indications that the father's absence or father's presence has an impact on the daughter's physiological development (e.g. menstruation). In father-absent homes, daughters are more likely to experience their menstrual cycle earlier in life than females from father-present homes. These findings then can be linked to sexual behaviors because it has also been shown that females who get their menstrual cycle earlier than females who get it later are at higher risk engaging in more sexual activity at an earlier age (Quinlan, 2003).

It is also important to point out that studies showed no consequential differences (i.e., sexual attitudes) between the father's presence and absence in the female's life when drawing a sample from a low socioeconomic status (SES) group (Crockett et al., 1993; Eberhardt and Schill, 1984). Conclusions can be drawn that adolescent females from a low SES seek early marriage or parenthood "as a means of escaping hardship and establishing an adult identity" (Rubin, 1976). A more positive outlook of engaging in sexual practices earlier in life can have an upside and is promoted in certain SES groups and cultures. Most of the research reviewed took a majority of the samples from Caucasian Western society, which does not leave much room for generalizing the findings of father-daughter relationships to all parts of the world

**Cognitive Functioning and School Performance**

Much literature on father-daughter relationships has been dedicated to the daughter's personality development and sexual conduct. Other research focuses on how the female can be affected by her dad's presence and absence through her academic achievement and performance. Father presence is seen to have positive affects on the daughter's intellectual development and social competence (Fagan & Iglesias, 1999). Other studies found that the absence of father affects the daughters' school performance more negatively than that of daughters' with a present dad (McLanahan & Teitler, 1999). Furthermore, well-fathered daughters tend to be more self-confident, self-reliant, and successful in school setting and in their professional careers than poorly-fathered daughters (Lamb, 1997; Amato 1994). These findings can be linked to the research to the daughter's self-esteem. As mentioned earlier, the presence of the father has positive effects on the daughter's self-esteem, which can be associated to better school performance. In support of self-esteem and academic performance, absent-fathers play a factor in the decline of well-being and academic achievement and cognitive ability of daughters (Johnson, 1996; Mulkey, Crain, & Harrington, 1992). Examples of these findings are seen in Table 2.

Table 2
*Effects of Father Presence of Daughter's Functioning*

| Presence of Father | Absence of Father |
|---|---|
| • Higher self-esteem<br>• Better school performance<br>• More assertive personality<br>• More responsible sexual behaviors<br>• Less likely to develop dependencies on men | • Lower self-esteem<br>• Lower school performance<br>• More likely to have permissive attitudes<br>• More likely to develop an eating disorder<br>• Engage in more sexual deviant behaviors<br>• More promiscuity<br>• More interpersonal problems<br>• More dependent on men |

**Summary**

Research has indicated that the presence and the absence of the father in the household reveal to have positive and negative consequences on the later development on the daughter. The role of the father is of great importance in the well-being of females, especially in her later development. More specifically, the father's role during childhood was positively related to the woman's educational and occupational mobility, psychological adjustment and well-being in adulthood (Amato, 1994). All research from the most original to the most current has revealed the importance of the fathers' role in a daughter's life. Table 2 shows how the presence and the absence of the father can impact certain areas of a females' life.

**Limitations Driving Research Elsewhere of Presence/Absence**

With four decades of work related to the significance of a father in his child's life, it is of curiosity that a void exists in the most simplistic form that can be studied. However, after a thorough examination of the literature available, it is clear that father involvement exists on a continuum and the valuable effects of being raised by a father depend on the quality of care they can provide (Jaffee, Moffitt, Caspi, & Taylor, 2003). For example, Jaffee et al. (2003) found that when fathers engaged in high levels of antisocial behavior, the more time they lived with their children, the more conduct problems their children had. This is indicative of more father involvement being less optimal in certain cases. With that awareness, it becomes more sensible as to why researchers have shunned away from basing any conclusions purely on whether father's live with their children or not. In other words, given that there is mainstream agreement among social scientists that fathers can be "absent" even when they reside with their children, and 'present" despite non-resident status, it seems reasonable that researchers may have been concerned that studying absence and presence in its most bare form would have led to criticism and/or disregard. Moreover, devoid an understanding of the potential value such a perceivably outdated review could have, such an examination lacked enthusiasm.

Recent research suggests that the impact of father absence flows through a subsequent course of presumptions that could explain results: 1) no co-parent, 2) economic loss / disadvantage, 3) social isolation and disapproval 4) perceived / actual abandonment relating to psychological distress, 5) conflict between parents (Cabrera, Tamis-LeMonda, Bradley, Hofferth, & Lamb, 2000). Since these may be the mechanisms (and not the presence or absence of a father) that create deleterious effects on children, it is of no wonder that researchers have spent their time investigating these elements and the moderators that can potentially slow or reverse harmful outcomes. To further drive research in the latter direction is the uncertainty over whether psychological and social well-being are needs obtained by a parent of a specific gender. Previous research maintains that a child's needs can be met with or without father involvement

(Walker & McGraw, 2000).

Davis and Friel (2001) proclaim the importance of moving beyond explorations of father presence or father absence as a result of recent research suggesting that family context, family process, patterns of interaction, and the quality of various relationships tend to have more explanatory power. All things considered however, the foundation for all research regarding father's influence comes from the findings that we have laid out throughout this review. Albeit the fact that one cannot reach conclusions about childhood outcomes based on data suggesting significant within-group distinctions, these distinctions have led to informed research of the contexts for which children in father present and father absent homes differ.

**Methodological Limitations in the Literature**

Overall, several limitations exist with how the construct of father presence and absence is conceptualized and measured, despite our best efforts to control for extraneous variables with more strict definitions. The most obvious measurement limitation in this fathering literature is that most of the studies are correlated. This makes inferring the direction of causality problematic and impossible to account for selection effects or pre-existing conditions inherent in the child that may have impacted child development outcomes (Pleck & Masciadrelli, 2004).

Undoubtedly it is important to consider measurement, sampling sizes, cultural and social class issues, to find better ways of understanding father presence than simply by directly comparing its opposite, father absence. One major limitation of the father present/absent literature is that most of the research is based on US population samples, of which African American samples represent a significant proportion of the father absence literature. The adverse child developmental outcomes reportedly due to father absence may, in part reflect the disadvantaged and disenfranchised experience of systemic and institutionalized racism rather than the impact of father absence. For example, Harper and McLanahan (2004) found that a sizeable portion of the risk attributed to father absence could actually be as a result of other factors such as, teen motherhood, low parent education, racial inequalities, and poverty. Furthermore, after controlling for socio-economic status, there were no differences found between children from single and two parent homes on measures of social skills and conflict management (Kesner & McKenry, 2001), educational achievement (Battle, 2002), and cognitive development (Averett, Gennetian, &Peters, 1997).

Due to the numerous types of measurements used, such as self-reports from the father or child, measurement from the mother, other relatives, schoolteachers and clinicians, they are subject to bias and errors. Additionally, virtually all the research has been cross-sectional and with each generational family structure changing so considerably, how one father's presence or absence affects his child may be radically different than another child he may abandon ten years later. This of course brings up the issue of moderators that also serve to complicate outcomes, including such things as, the personality of the child, the coping styles of the child, and the level of stress and warmth of the mother with the list going on to even such moderators as owning a pet. Thus, it becomes obvious that research in this arena is complicated and because of its ever changing dynamic, a clear picture of the role of a father in his son or daughter's life will always be convoluted matter.

**Discussion of Literature**

To summarize the considerable information reviewed in this chapter, the following five questions and answers can guide or provide a context for interpreting this literature.

*1. What types of research have been reported on a father's role in his child's development over the last four decades?*

Once research began to reveal the significance of the father's role in his child's development, there was an explosion of research. It began with research similar to what was presented here by looking at children who grew up with fathers present as compared with children growing up without fathers in the home. A problem though, was that the operational definitions used at the time were vague decreasing the strength of the positive correlations found; however, not wasting any time, researchers began developing studies in order to determine the causes of the positive correlations found. The research corresponded with the mainstream view of a father's role, beginning with the father as a moral teacher, then as the breadwinner, to the sex-role model, to the supportive husband, and finally to the warmth and care of the father. With so many variables to look at and so many potential confounding variables, it is difficult for researchers to keep up with the rapidly changing family dynamics of our time.

*2. What types of literature were reviewed for this study?*

Due to the operational definitions used to describe present and absent fathers, most of the literature for this review has come from correlational studies, particularly ones that looked at father absence, single parent families, and divorced families. Since it would be unethical to control for the independent variable (whether the father is present or absent), we used descriptive operational definitions. Although this restricted our ability to determine causation, it reduced the extraneous variables that weakened many of the correlations found in the past.

*3. What predictions can be made about boy's simply based on the presence or absence of their father? And, what predictions can be made about girl's simply based on the presence or absence of their father?*

Due to the profound differential effects that fathers have on their sons and daughters it made sense to keep the bodies of research separate. Since most prior research has either been focused solely on boys or on both genders together, we are taking this opportunity to combine what we have observed regarding sons and daughters as a means to summarize our findings as a brief comparison. Reviewing the culmination of research, we found that children of absent fathers (both boys and girls) have an increased risk for greater and earlier sexual activity, dramatically greater risk of drug and alcohol abuse, more mental illness, more suicide, poorer educational performance, and higher rates of teen pregnancy, criminality, and sexual abuse. Breaking that down separately, boys are more likely to suffer child abuse and more often have an earlier death. Boys also appear to experience more confused identities, more aggressive behavior, more antisocial behavior, and more school suspensions than their gender counterparts. Girls on the other hand tend to experience greater emotional distress, more anxiety, and more depression than boys.

*4. What limitations have prevented researchers from such a straightforward look at a father's role in his sons or daughters development?*

With the burgeoning information that has been realized since the quest to discover the magnitude of a father's role on his children's development, it has been difficult for researchers to keep up. Soon after noting that children with absent fathers fared worse than those with present fathers, researchers began to look for reasons and considered the limitations of those studies insignificant.

Furthermore, during this time began the crises over limits of the scientific method in social psychology that resulted from many of the post WWII studies, such as Milgrim's obedience research (Richard, Bond, & Stokes-Zoota, 2003). This brought on a growing interest in developing ways to scientifically study human behavior in an ethical manner. This encouraged researchers to abandon correlation work, in favor of controlling studies, that would specify why a father was important.

**Definition of Terms**

In order to accurately understand this study's focus and direction, the following relevant terms are defined.

1) *Fatherlessness*: This aspect of the family dynamic will be defined, for the purposes of this research, as an individual who grew up in a home without face to face contact with his father for a minimum of five years.

2) *Perception*: What does the individual think about the reason of his father's absence.

3) *Positive perception of father*: An individual who exhibits love, warmth, sympathy or caring towards their absent father.

4) *Negative perception of father*: An individual who exhibits anger, resentment, hate, frustration, or disgust towards their absent father.

5) *Neutral perception of father*: An individual who exhibits no feelings, or who is indifferent, towards their absent father.

6) *Processing*: working through his feelings.

# CHAPTER III

## Method

### Research Design

A qualitative approach was in the data collection process. The qualitative nature of the study took a phenomenological method of inquiry, which connected data to current research, and identified gaps within the body of knowledge on paternal absence. A phenomenological approach was used to understand the experiences of adults in regards to their perceptions, and its development, of their absent fathers. Understanding this phenomenon required the researcher to implement an exploratory and emergent design. As more data was collected, the research questions often shifted to focus on the specific experiences of the participants' disclosure.

Patton (2002) explained how phenomenological strategies combined with exploratory and emergent designs, for purpose of qualitative data, allow a researcher to obtain an in-depth understanding of the experiences of the population being studied. He also goes further to explain that the quality of qualitative data depends to a great extent on the methodological skill, sensitivity and integrity of the researcher. Furthermore, the overall purpose of qualitative research is to provide a clear and in depth conceptualization of individuals/community experiences. (Patton 2002).

The researcher compared present data to data within current and past research in order to identify new themes and categories of the phenomenon. This method consisted of comparing and contrasting data obtained in the present study to studies described in the literature review that focused on paternal absence. The researcher looked for themes that were specific to males from ages 18-35 years, allowing a clearer understanding of a specific population's experience to emerge. These data were collected through interviews and observations of participants who have met the research inclusion criteria.

The researcher interviewed adults who were raised without a father in the home. In other words, the participants were raised by a mother, aunt, uncle, older sibling, grandparents etc. Despite the overwhelming amount of research focusing on children without fathers, this research addressed the phenomenon from an individualistic approach, rather than by exploring group dynamics. This research took away the paternal factor and focused on the mental process of his son.

Due to the possibility that saturation was not met because of gender specific experiences, only males were included in the study. A separate study would be required to examine this phenomenon from a female's perspective

Understanding the development and transition of an individual's negative/positive/neutral perception, especially in the area of absent fathers, has social and clinical relevance due to the prevalence of absent fathers. Furthermore, this study attempted to give an in depth understanding of how family perceptions are formed and maintained. Using an exploratory and emergent design study to address this phenomenon also allowed the researcher freedom to create new frameworks in relation to the initial research question.

**Participants**

Purposeful sampling was utilized to select participants who had significant information on the phenomenon under study. Patton (2002) describes this type of population as samples within samples and suggests that purposeful samples can be "stratified or nested by selecting particular units or cases that vary according to a key dimension." For qualitative research studies, the saturation effect is reached by a certain amount of participants; however, considering resources and time limitations this research only had 8 to 10 participants.

Furthermore, due to the time constraints, a convenience sample was sought to maximize time and resources. Even so, a maximum variation method of sampling was also considered in order to document diverse variations that emerge in adapting to different conditions. This type of sampling helped to identify important and common patterns across participants (Patton 2002). The participants will include 9 men with an age range of 21-35 years. The sample for this research will include Caucasian, African American, and Mexican American males who were raised without a father from childhood. All of the participants were born and raised in Southern California and varied in aspects surrounding; education, socioeconomic status, relationships, offspring, and beliefs surrounding themselves and their environment.

**Inclusion Criteria**

Participants must have had an absent father at any time in their childhood or adolescence (ages 0-18 years). In this study, the reason for the father's absence was not relevant for exclusion. Any situation regarding the father's absence (e.g., death, military service, imprisonment, divorce, separation, surrogacy, lesbian relationships, work, relocation, and issues surrounding immigration) was allowed participation in the study. It was important to identify perceptional patterns within similar or alternate reasons for paternal absence. Paternal absence was defined as not having contact with a father for at least five years.

**Exclusion Criteria**

Persons who were raised with a father in the home were excluded. Also persons who presented as psychotic, severely depressed, suicidal, or homicidal were excluded from the study.

The participants were asked (by the researcher) if they were currently experiencing any hallucinatory, depressive, and suicidal or homicidal symptoms. Exclusion criteria was assessed by examining responses and the demographics questionnaire (Appendix D). Participants who endorse depression, suicidal ideation, homicidal ideation psychosis, or severe drug use were excluded from the study and given a referral for treatment of their symptoms.

**Materials**

The materials in this study consisted of one audio tape recorder. In the Informed Consent (Appendix B) participants gave permission to be audio taped.

**Measures**

Two measures were used in this study; a semi-structured interview guide and a demographics questionnaire, described below.

**Semi-Structured Interview Guide (SSIG)**

The semi-structured questionnaire consisted of 10 open-ended questions that addressed each participant's perception, and its development, of his absent father. These questions addressed current perceptions which were retrospective in nature to identify past emotions and cognitions. The interview guide was evaluated by a Proposal Development pre-doctoral class of five, and the researcher's chairperson. The style of questioning was heavily influenced by research on people's individual perception and feelings surrounding family dynamics (See Appendix A).

The researcher asked participants to respond to questions on the SSIG verbally. The participants were also asked to take a narrative approach in describing their experience as open and honest as possible; including everything that may be relevant. The participants were made aware of their ability to share as much or as little as they want regarding their perception and experience with an absent father. The researcher also assured the participants that the quality of this study was related to their responses validity. Participants were given the opportunity to decline to answer specific questions if they feel uncomfortable; however, such behaviors were noted in the results section as a factor related to their experience.

**Demographics**

A demographics form was given to the participant before the interview began. Each participant was asked to describe their age, education history, socioeconomic status, parental status, relationship status, and alcohol/drug use. Participants who currently used (not dependent) drugs or alcohol were admitted into the study. These participants were admitted into the study due to the hypothesis that their substance use may have potentially had relevance to existing perceptions of their absent fathers.

Such data were used to identify aspects of their lives that might not be covered in the SSIG. The demographics form was also used to clarify information regarding the population that was being studied. This questionnaire gathered information regarding mean age, education level, and socioeconomic status, marital status, drug use, and employment status. The demographics form was also used to report if the participants were, at the time, parents and if they were married or are in a relationship. This data may also be used for future research related to the perceptions of absent fathers.

For the purpose of assessing exclusion criteria, potential participants were asked if they were currently taking any medication for depression. Patients were also asked if they were taking any anti-psychotic medication and if they felt depressed, homicidal, suicidal, or have any psychotic symptoms (See Appendix E).

## Procedure

Participants for this research were recruited through email, posted flyers, and word of mouth. The emails which request participation were sent to all graduate students at Alliant International University (California School of Professional Psychology, San Diego). Flyers were also posted throughout Alliant's San Diego campus: library, student lounge, cafeteria, and classrooms and living facilities. A phone number was supplied on the flyer so that the participants could contact the researcher. All potential participants contacted the researcher via phone or email. A twenty dollar gift card was used as an incentive for allowing the researcher to interview the participant, each participant received one.

Participants were assessed for inclusion criteria over the phone. They were asked to describe their family structure from the earliest point they can remember. Exclusion criteria were assessed through the demographics questionnaire.

Participants did not meet each other due to data quality. The research may have been contaminated if different perceptions of absent fathers influence one another. The researcher and participants met in a confidential/comfortable setting that the participant suggested (e.g. their residence). If the participant did not have a preference, the interviews were be conducted on the first floor of Alliant International University's (San Diego) library or within a Los Angeles Public Library.

At the time, the researcher began each interview by building rapport with the participants. He also worked on creating an alliance which facilitated an environment that allowed the participants' disclosure to be safely expressed. The participants were be given the questionnaire prior to the initial interview. Since much of the questionnaire is retrospective in manner, the participants may have needed more time to remember their past experience, thus they were asked to read the questionnaire prior to the initial interview.

The participants were informed of their rights in reference to this research. They were asked to sign a form that explained such rights, they had the right to: disclose as much or as little as they desire, confidentiality, withdraw from the study at any time, see the results of their data, and therapeutic treatment post interview.

The interview was one hour to one hour and thirty minutes long. Post interview, the participant were be debriefed by the researcher regarding the purpose of the study and its clinical implications. If the research material caused any participant emotional or psychological distress, a list of referrals were given to assist with any post-participation problems. However, the interviewer assured the participant was not a danger to self or others.

After the interview, the participants were contacted one week later to inquire of their emotional and psychological well-being. They were be thanked and reassured of the nature of confidentiality within the study. Regarding this research, the tape recordings and transcripts will be kept for seven years and then destroyed.

**Provisions of Trustworthiness**

To provide qualitative research that is valid and understandable to read, the researcher took steps to ensure the study is conducted with an audit trail. The researcher kept a journal of thoughts, experiences and questions that arose within the study. The researcher also consulted with his dissertation chair, reader, and dissertation class of peers regarding the questionnaire, research topic, question, current literature, and data collection process.

A proposal, memos, and data analysis were conducted while in consultation with the dissertation committee. The second provision of trustworthiness came from the participant. The participants were given the transcripts after the interview to ensure accuracy of their communicated experience.

# CHAPTER IV

## Results

### Participants' Background Information

The 9 participants in this study were recruited via email, posted flyers, and word of mouth. The flyers were posted at Alliant International University (California School of Professional Psychology, San Diego). Flyers were posted throughout Alliant's San Diego campus: library, student lounge, cafeteria, and classrooms and living facilities. An invitation to participate in the study was also sent to a vast audience using the social media tool Facebook.

All 9 of the interviews were conducted in person. At the time of the interviews participants' information varied in socioeconomic status, employment, marital status, parental status, education, ethnicity, income and time at which their father left the home more detailed information can be found within the demographic table below.

Table 3: Demographic Information

| Participant | Age | Ethnicity | Relationship Status | Highest Education Completed | Number of Children | Mental Health Issues | Age When Father Left the Home |
|---|---|---|---|---|---|---|---|
| Robert | 30 | Latino | Domestic Partnership | Middle School | 1 | None | 10 |
| Jonathan | 33 | African American | Engaged | College | 3 | None | 10 |
| William | 28 | Latino | Single | High School | 1 | Depression | 2 |
| Steve | 28 | Latino | Married | High School | 0 | None | Before Birth |
| Ruben | 28 | Latino | Engaged | High School | 1 | None | 10 |
| Ravon | 30 | African American | Single | High School | 0 | None | 1 |
| Mike | 28 | African American | Single | College | 0 | None | 2 |
| Paul | 33 | Mexican American | Single | Graduate School | 0 | None | 13 |
| Eloy | 27 | Indian/ Mexican | Single | College | 0 | None | 1 |

## Description of Participants

The following section includes a brief history of each participant which illustrates the participant and their behavior during the interview process.

<u>Participant 1: Robert</u>

Robert is a large built man who played high school and college football. His stature towers over other individuals. However, his intimidating physical presence is quickly minimized by his candid personality and warm smile. He is a 30 year old Latino unemployed male who was recently released from jail due to pleading no contest to an auto theft charge. During the interview, Robert exhibited fragmented perceptions of self. Throughout the interview he showed conflicting views of himself, his feelings, and his understanding of his father. Robert knew his father was a drug addict and was arrested for possession of narcotics. He was very angry and used words like "pissed" to explain his perceptions of his father. However, Robert readily tried to defend and justify his father's actions and absence in a positive manner. He said, "My dad was a drug addict but not one of those you see on skid row." This social comparison of his father to homeless drug addicts allowed him to feel better about his father and the negative perception that plagued his thoughts.

The conflicting perceptions of his father led to conflicting feelings towards his absence. He was very angry at his father but had trouble expressing this anger. He said things like, "I am mad because he is not here because of the shit he has done." However, there was an underlining desire to change these feelings he has for his father. He does not want to be angry at him, but he cannot help holding resentment for the feelings of abandonment. This unachieved attempt to change his feelings has caused him much pain. He said, "I don't like talking about the shit he has done it hurts." Until now, the participant has chosen to hide from these feelings and internalize their effect.

Such internalization has caused him to have conflicting views of his own self-perception. The participant felt he wasn't worth anything and verbalized that he is not what a man should be. He exhibited signs of self-loathing and hatred of what and who he is. This phenomenon is a result of the conflict between his understanding and feelings of his father, which has been directed inward, causing the participant to hate himself.

Consistent with the prior conflicts, Robert also showed positive aspects of himself. The participant explained himself to be a likeable person, a good friend, and someone with lots of love. There are conflicting cognitions, ideas, and emotions throughout the participant's experience as seen in earlier negative views of self. Robert's behaviors are similarly related to his conflicting perceptions as they are to his absent father.

When Robert was a child, he exhibited deviant behaviors in the absence of his father. He knew his father was in prison and exhibited such behaviors similar to the findings of Fritsch and Burkhead. Their study demonstrated that it is not father absence, per se, that correlates with problematic behavior in children, but rather the combination of father absence and the knowledge that they are absent due to imprisonment (Fritsch & Burkhead, 1981).

Robert knew his father was in jail and the reason he was arrested; this knowledge was just as much of an impact on him as the absence of his father.

Participant 2: Jonathan

Jonathan is also a very large male. He stands 6 feet 7 inches and towers over the majority of people he interacts with. Jonathan was a scholarship basketball player at the University of

Southern California who was recruited out of New York; where he grew up. After college, he played basketball with various teams including one in Puerto Rico and one in Europe. Jonathan's dominating demeanor does not reflect his soft spoken and gentle temperament. He is warm hearted and easily considers the feelings and perspective of others.

This was evident by observing behaviors during the interview. Jonathan asked to conduct the interview for this study in his home where the researcher could observe his interactions with his family. He offered seating and beverages to his guest and was constantly attentive of the needs of those around him.

Jonathan's explanation of his experience without a father allows the researcher to understand how he has coped and developed. His father left the home when he was 10 years of age. With no explanation, Jonathan found himself confused and concerned about the wellbeing of his family and father. Throughout his childhood, Jonathan also found himself missing school and exhibiting explosive behaviors. During this time, he utilized basketball as a way to cope with his misunderstood feelings of not having a father. He pursued basketball and became extremely successful with such an outlet. He currently has 3 children, 2 of which are in New York, and he has some contact with them. Jonathan recently had a baby girl and a fiancée who he currently lives with.

Jonathan's lack of understanding about his father, the absence, and their relationship is seen in his behaviors. He is highly aware of his environment and interpersonal interactions.

However, there is some lack of insight into his thoughts and feelings. Jonathan struggles to explain his feelings and connections between his behavior and internal processes. He projects the appearance that he does not really care nor wants to search for his father. However, his behaviors contradict this self-perpetuated perception. He has searched for his father on the internet and has asked his family about his father's whereabouts. He portrays as a strong and in control man and defends words and actions in order to decrease looking vulnerable, which he believes to be an undesirable trait.

Participant 3: William

William is a Mexican American male who currently lives in Los Angeles. William asked to be interviewed in his home due to feeling it would be a safe place for him to describe his experiences without a father. Upon introduction, William met the researcher on the street and walked him into his home where a group of children played with an old dog in their front yard. William was eager to discuss his experience as he immediately began talking before the researcher sat down. As he was redirected from his disclosure to fill out the demographics questionnaire, William addressed questions regarding some exclusion criteria. He explained how he once was depressed and suicidal. He also had once experienced psychotic symptoms and was hospitalized. William reported he has not experienced depression, suicidal ideation, or psychotic symptoms within the past year. This information allowed his further participation in the research study.

William speaks very fast and becomes tangential at times when he discloses emotional arousing information. He often speaks in metaphors and very frequently uses vulgarities in his speech. His morbid comparisons to his life experiences are consistent with his external appearance. William is a self-identified "Goth" who wears all black attire associated with such an identity. William's eccentric piercings weigh down his ear and lip as the heavy metals stretch his bronze skin.

William's experiences without a father weigh heavily on his mood and are reportedly "causes" for much of his failures. William describes his father with conflicting ideas which have the potential to create dissonance. He reports significant anger and "rage" towards his father, but has the desire to connect with him and reestablish a father-son relationship. William's rage is justified by childhood abuse that he experienced; he believes the continuously violating childhood experience could have been avoided if his father was present. William blames his father "for not protecting" him during this time of his life, he also reports more anger towards his father than to the perpetrator.

During the interview the researcher was able to identify some instability in William's mood and psychological functioning. This type of behavior is consistent with individuals who have suffered childhood abuse. Much of the instability and strong emotional arousal are directed towards his father and is reportedly, "to blame for the way I am."
William's son has been a contributing factor to help him understand and process his own experience. He has difficulty being physically affectionate with others even to the point where he had trouble hugging his own son. William has been able to work through such feelings and reports a strong bond with his son.

During the interview he was open and seemed genuine, his personality "is one that takes time to understand" but his warmth and genuineness are traits that make him a much desirable individual. He explained that he acts and dresses in a certain way to keep people away; and reports he does not trust people who try to get close to him. This way, he "is able to filter out those who are not looking understand the real William."

Participant 4: Steve

Steve is a short and stalky 28 year old Mexican American male. He is currently married with no children and resides in East Los Angeles. Steve currently works for an armored transporting service as an armed guard. Prior to the interview for this research, Steve exhibited strong interest in discussing his feelings regarding his absent father. He was very flexible and opted to meet the researcher wherever was convenient.

Steve is a family oriented individual who grew up with his mother and 2 brothers. At a young age he had to find a job and help financially support his family. He explains thinking about his life and wondering "if it would have taken a different road" if his father were around. He explained how he would have loved to follow his dreams, but was deterred by having to grow up very fast.

Steve's father left the home before he was born. He explains his father's absence as an affair that ended up in his mother becoming pregnant. One component of his parent's early affair appeared to significantly distress Steve; as it was apparent during the interview. His father gave his mother 10 thousand dollars to either abort the unplanned pregnancy, or raise the child alone; either way Steve's father immediately left. This thought plagues him on a daily basis, he is upset with the idea that his life was once monetarily valued.

Steve has never met his father but has once seen him. His aunt identified him; and at that moment he noticed a change in his behavior and thinking. He reported becoming more aggressive and had outbursts at home and school. He also started to feel depressed. Steve was under the impression that his father was dead, he became confused and frustrated when this thought was contradicted. At an early age he "could not understand why his father could be alive and not be in his life."

Currently, Steve is curious about this father and has a desire to reconnect and establish a relationship. Early in his childhood and adolescence, he exhibited resentment and anger towards his absent father. However, as an adult, Steve shows an absence of anger replaced by curiosity and understanding.

Participant 5: Ruben

Ruben is a twenty-eight year old Mexican American who has one son. Ruben currently lives with his son and fiancée in a 1 bedroom apartment in the city of Los Angeles. He is a 6 foot 3 inch former football player who currently coaches little league football. Ruben also works as a teacher for children who have learning disabilities and require special services.

Upon meeting Ruben, it was clear that he is a very bright and intelligent individual. He spoke in an eloquent manner utilizing his experience as a reference for his work with children. Similarly, he explored his experience of having a son which helped to change his perception and feelings towards his absent father.

Furthermore, Ruben discussed a familial cycle of paternal absence within his lineage. His father's father was absent similar to Ruben's childhood experience. This dynamic also allowed Ruben to further understand and express empathy for his father. It also played a major role in the first year of Ruben becoming a father. Paradoxically, Ruben became afraid he would perpetuate the family cycle of failing as a father, this fear, reportedly, caused him to leave his responsibilities and abandon his son. Over time, he became cognizant of his behavior and reluctantly decided to return and father his son. Ruben reports this to be "the best decision of his life."

Ruben's older brother, Paul, is also a participant in this research. Their participation helps to explain that the same situation can be experienced and understood in various ways. The two participants were interviewed separately and both were very interested in learning their brother's experience.

Ruben is the youngest son of the three male children in his family. He reported his father left the family for another woman, whom he eventually had children with. He also reported that his father later died of health problems in the spring of 2001. Ruben explained different feelings towards the occasions where his father left; once he left the family, the other he left the "earth." His experience helped to highlight variations of perception and understanding, when compared to his brother's disclosure; regarding their father leaving the home versus passing away.

When Ruben's father left, he became the son who provided emotional support for his mother. He would often spend nights with his mother, consoling her till she was able to sleep. His two older brothers served different roles as a consequence of their father's absence; which is further explained in Paul's "participant description."

Participant 6: Paul

Paul had a different experience than his younger brother. In the interview, Paul described his thoughts and feelings relevant to his father leaving the home. When his father left, he contemplated dropping out of school due to its impact on the family's finances. Paul immediately had to find work to help his mother, consequently, his grades were impacted and his "life was altered." As a promising basketball player and outstanding student he realized that his plans for college may be strayed by alterations in family dynamics. Paul became parentified as he took on the role of the provider for the family; he worked nights and went to school in the day time. Such transition in roles induced resentment directed at his absent father. Although his adolescence took a different path than he had planned, he was eventually admitted into the University of California, Los Angeles where he graduated with a bachelor's degree and has recently completed a master's degree. He is currently a high school teacher and a basketball coach who is single and has no children.

The resentment towards his father remains consistent as Paul describes his current feelings. His father passed away in 2001 and he recalls "feeling nothing" towards the death. He reported, "I don't wish death on anyone but I am not broken up about my father dying." Paul "wishes no ill will" towards his father or his memory, but he has become "numb" thinking about his situation as an adolescent.

Participant 7: Ravon

Ravon is a thirty year old African American male who works as a lost prevention officer at a retail store. He currently lives in Los Angeles with his mother, grandmother, 2 sisters and 2 younger cousins. The researcher was contacted by Ravon over the telephone; he reported seeing a flyer for the study on a university campus. During the conversation Ravon expressed his interest in the research and asked to meet at a Starbucks coffee shop in downtown Los Angeles.

When the researcher arrived to the agreed upon site, Ravon had already been waiting. Confidentiality became an issue due to the nature of the location where he had asked to meet. The researcher and Ravon sat at a table where bikes, cars, and college students passed. The excessive commotion made it difficult to hear, especially since Ravon is a soft spoken individual.

He presented as a muscular man who stood about 6 feet and dressed in casual clothes. As the interview began, the researcher noticed Ravon's style of responding to the interview questions to be different from other participants. He often utilized single word answers to respond to questions that required elaboration. The researcher utilized prompts to get a further in-depth understanding of Ravon's experience, but he struggled to share more than what was minimally required. His father left the home when Ravon was 1 year old, which reflected much of his ambivalence during the interview.

He had no memories of his father nor did he know the reason that his father left the family. Ravon expressed no form resentment or anger towards his father; in fact, he discussed no feelings at all towards his father or his absence. During his childhood he saw the majority of his peers grow up without a paternal presence. He stated, "No one I knew when I was growing up had a father, I thought that was just the way it was supposed to be…it would have been weird if I had a dad really…not having a dad was normal…I didn't realize it until I would watch shows like the Cosby's and see what a family is supposed to be like."

Ravon's disclosed experience reflects internal psychological processes. He did not know much about his father and when asked, "What makes a good father?" Ravon could not answer. The same lack of understanding applied to the questions "What makes a man," "Can you describe your feelings towards your father's absence," and "Has your father's absence played a role in your life?" He could not answer these questions and stated, "I just don't know."

Participant 8: Mike

Mike is a twenty-eight year old African American male who currently lives with his girlfriend in a large city in Southern California. Mike is a former college football player who attempted to play in the National Football League, but was circumstantially redirected to another field of work.  He is currently finishing a master's in business administration (MBA) in accounting, and he also mentors inner city children who have come from rough neighborhoods and broken families. His work with these children allows him to, "Give back to kids whom he can understand and hopefully make difference in their lives."

Mike was eager to participate in this research and to share his experience without his father. He invited the researcher to his home to conduct the interview. Upon introduction, Mike greeted the researcher with a large smile and a complimenting embrace. He presented as a large built man with a muscular frame and caramel colored skin. Sprinkled throughout his face and much of his upper body lie hundreds of freckles which he reported to, "Once be insecure over…but eventually was able to get over them and accept himself for who he is."

Mike's father left the home when he was 2 years old. His father was a drug dealer who became addicted to crack cocaine and heroin, of which came various legal problems, and caused him to be in and out of prison. Mike's father is currently incarcerated with a life sentence due to a violent offense which involved a deadly weapon. During the interview, Mike became tearful as he explained feelings surrounding his father's aggressive actions, and his belief, that his father will never be released from prison. Mike has often thought about visiting his father but has always come to the same conclusion, "Why should I be a part of his life now, when he had the chance to be a part of mine, but was never there for me when I needed him?"

Mike reports having dealt with anger directed towards his father as a child. He explains feeling different towards his father now when compared to his childhood, adolescence, and early adult life. He discussed memories of his father, which include significant neglect, that impacted his childhood as well as the way he understood himself (as seen in Major Theme 5). Mike "had to learn how to take care of himself early because he knew his father was not going to be there and his mother was always working."

During much of the interview Mike was open and shared his experience in depth. He seemed engaged and maintained good eye contact. However, when Mike's girlfriend walked into the living room where he and the researcher were conducting the interview, there was a noticeable shift in his demeanor and style of disclosure. He immediately sat back in his chair, crossed his legs, and altered the tone in his voice. Upon her entrance, Mike began to show little emotion and minimized the impact of his father's absence; when compared to how he behaved and the nature of his disclosure before she entered. This may be evidence that Mike has worked on preserving an image around himself and his relationship regarding his feelings towards his father.

<u>Participant 9: Eloy</u>

Eloy is a 27 year old male who is half Mexican and half Indian; he presents with a small body frame and projects a casual and pleasant demeanor. He stood 5 feet 7 inches and spoke in a rushed and tangential manner. Eloy tended to discuss his experience through the use of metaphors and examples which took extended amounts of time to convey. He currently works as a player development agent for the National Football League and has aspirations of becoming a general manager for a professional football team. Eloy asked to meet the researcher, three houses away from his home; where he currently lives with his mother. Eloy expressed feeling "embarrassed, because his house was disorganized."

When the researcher arrived, Eloy greeted him and introduced other members of the home where the interview would be taking place. It appeared as if he had a strong relationship with the individuals who lived in the home as he introduced them as "family;" however, they were of no blood relation. Eloy explained that he sees family as "those I can trust" and "people who won't abandon me when I need them."

His father left the home when Eloy was 1 year old. Eloy explained the nature of his father's absence, was due to cultural differences, which forced his father to leave his family and return to India. Eloy's Indian grandmother disapproved of her son marrying anyone outside of their culture. She told Eloy's father, "he was disgracing the family and she would disown him if he proceeded with the unarranged relationship.' Eloy's father decided to leave his American family and return to India where he currently has a family and 3 children.

Although his father paid child support and allowed Eloy to be covered under his health insurance, the family fell under extreme financial difficulty. During much of his childhood, Eloy lived in a trailer home and had to use public toilets as well as bath in restaurant sinks. This caused Eloy much resentment directed at his mother. He thought she could have "done something different to keep his father in the home" and blamed their financial difficulties upon her. Eloy explained, "It took therapy as well as soul searching to understand that I was angry at my father but I put it on my mom...he wasn't around so I could not blame him for the way we lived." He further explained his frustration was eventually transferred to his father which then became anger. Eloy's discussed hating himself and the Indian culture because they both reminded him of his father. At age 18, he was able to legally change his last name, consequently, "severing any ties to his father."

Overtime, the anger he felt dissolved as he began to "understand" and "challenge irrational beliefs" about what it meant to grow up without a father as well as the reason why his father left their family. Eloy initially believed he was not a "good enough son" and his father did not want him. However, Eloy began to discuss his experience with his mother and other family members, who helped him understand the reason his father was not in his life.

During the interview, Eloy explained a significant experience that changed his perception of his father, and thus, changed the way he felt about himself. Around age 18, Eloy came across a box of letters from his father explaining cultural dynamics which caused his absence. He also read "how much his father loved and cared for him." This event changed the way Eloy felt about his experience as a child and his beliefs surrounding his father.

### Categories and Themes

The purpose of the present study was to gain a better understanding of individuals experience and perception of their absent father. Data that was collected during the interviews was analyzed using the constant comparative method. This method requires the researcher to code the data into units of meaning (Maykut & Morehouse, 1994). Similar units of meaning are grouped together which develop into categories that represent themes within the data (Maykut & Morehouse, 1994). For the present study, categories were first developed and then themes were created by placing participants' statements together that maintained similar ideas relevant to their experience of being raised without a father.

Throughout the interview, four categories and twenty-two themes were identified as relevant to the participants experience without a father emerged. These themes were established by the researcher accompanied by the collaboration of his dissertation committee. These themes categorized the overall experience and perception of growing up without a father that the participants described during the interviews.

The four categories identified include: the experience of growing up without a father, perceptions of paternal absence, feelings towards father, and coping without a father. From these categories, twenty-two themes emerged from the data which included; 1) Relationships with Mother, 2) Discussions about Absent Father, 3) Childhood Experience without a Father: Parentification, 4) Childhood Behaviors, 5) Significant Memories of Father, 6) Current Feelings towards Father: a) Displacement b) Processing, 7) Current Desire for One's Father, 8) Changes Perceptions and Feelings, 9) Current Perception of Father's Absence, 10) Feelings Regarding Father's Absence, 11) Perceived Effects Related to Father's Absence: Motivation, 12)Feelings of Self: a) The Cycle b) Avoiding Self Hatred, 13) Parenting: The Importance of Paternal Modeling, 14) Understanding the Male Role, 15) Talking about Absent Father, 16) What Makes Family, 17) Childhood Feelings towards Father, 18) Significant Adults who were Supportive, 19) Experiences in School, 20) Acquired Values Related to Absent Father, 21) Connecting with Absent Father, 22) Father's Day.

Table 4: Categories and Themes  *Participant (P)

| Categories | P#1 | P#2 | P#3 | P#4 | P#5 | P#6 | P#7 | P#8 | P#9 |
|---|---|---|---|---|---|---|---|---|---|
| The experience of growing up without a father | X | X | X | X | X | X | X | X | X |
| Perceptions of paternal absence | X | X | X | X | X | X | X | X | X |
| Feelings towards father | X | X | X | X | X | X | X | X | X |
| Coping without a father | X | X | X | X | X | X | X | X | X |
| **Themes** | | | | | | | | | |
| Relationships with Mother | X | X | X | X | X | X | X | X | X |
| Discussions about Absent Father | X | X | X | X | X | X | X | X | X |
| Childhood Experience without a Father: Parentification/Defenses | X | X | X | X | X | X | X | X | X |
| Childhood Behaviors | X | X | X | X | X | X | X | | X |
| Significant Memories of Father | X | X | X | X | X | X | X | X | |
| Dynamics of Current Feelings towards Father | X | X | X | X | X | X | X | X | X |
| Current Desire for One's Father | | X | X | X | X | X | X | X | X |
| Changes in Perceptions and Feelings | X | X | X | X | X | | X | X | X |
| Current Perception of Father's Absence | X | X | X | X | X | X | X | X | X |
| Feelings Regarding Father's Absence | X | X | X | X | X | | X | X | X |
| Perceived Effects Related to Father's Absence: Motivation | X | | X | X | X | X | X | X | X |
| Feelings of Self: Maladaptive Cycle and Avoiding Self Hatred | | | X | X | X | X | X | X | X |
| Parenting: The Importance of Paternal Modeling | X | X | X | X | X | X | X | X | |
| Understanding the Male Role | X | X | X | X | X | | X | X | X |
| Experience while Talking about Absent Father | | X | X | X | X | X | X | X | X |
| What Makes Family | | X | | X | X | X | X | X | X |
| Childhood Feelings towards Father | X | X | X | | X | | X | X | | X |
| Significant Adults who were Supportive | X | X | X | X | | X | X | X | |
| Experiences in School | X | X | X | X | | | X | | X |
| Acquired Values Related to Absent Father | | X | X | | | | X | X | X |
| Connecting with Absent Father | | X | X | X | X | | X | X | X |
| Father's Day | | | | X | X | X | X | X | X |

## Description of Themes and Supporting Quotations

Category One: The Experience of Growing up without a Father

The following six themes within this category emerged from the interviews.

Theme One: Relationships with Mother

When asked to describe their experience growing up without their fathers; many of the participants discussed their relationship with their mother. Some of the relationships were strengthened due to the absence of their father but others became distant and difficult to manage.

Jonathan: "My mother and I, we have a good relationship. No problems, never argue never have disagreements. It was good when I was a child to. I was always a good kid, besides being a brat and missing school."

Willy: "In every one's eyes...your vision becomes skewed for what you want to see...but in my eyes there really wasn't a relationship with my mom. After she left my dad she was a youngster so she would try to catch up on her mid-twenties. They would drag her home some nights piss drunk and that's all I remember. All the clubs that she likes...to me, working at the club is my way of fighting off my daemons from her... because I was there controlling what she used to be...I made it harder for people like her to come out. I do have a relationship with my mom but the damage of the past is done."

Robert: "My relationship with my mom is weird. Like um, we love each other but we don't show it a lot. You know?"

Theme Two: Discussions about Absent Father

Participants experience varied in terms of discussing their father's absence with family members and friends. Talking about their father's absence, be it; not talking at all or continuously asking questions, was a theme within these participants experience. It is evident that the participants' perception of their father's absence was influenced by these early discussions; they were asked, "Was there ever a discussion about your father being gone?"

Steve:      "My mom told me that he had a family on the side. When my mom told him that she was pregnant he said, "Here is Ten thousand dollars, go take care of it." Ten grand later, I'm still here and his money is no where to be found. She made the right decision…I have accomplished a lot. I have nothing to prove to him. I am married, I have a decent job. But I hated that he thought he could get rid of me for 10 thousand dollars, that's all I was worth to him? As a child I never really asked about my father because I was so used to living without one. I started asking about him when I knew he was alive."

Ruben:      "I wouldn't necessarily say there was ever a discussion about my father's absence. When my mom would talk to me about my dad I would block it out."

Ravon:      "No, there was never a real discussion about my dad. I mean they talked about him but it was like where is he at? They wouldn't really talk much about him, just how he used to be back in the day. No real details. It wasn't till I became older until I started to learn about who he really was."

Paul:       "Not immediately when he left but eventually there was a discussion about my father. I was encouraging my mother to meet people and date so she wouldn't be alone. But she has not and she will not. So we didn't really talk about him, more just how she should forget about him."

Theme Three: Childhood Experience without a Father: Parentification and Defenses

Each participant shared their experience growing up in a single parent home. They described adopting new roles when their father left; some becoming parentified. Participants also discussed ways they managed their feelings and behaviors through the implementation of psychological defenses, which helped them manage their experience.

Willy: "I don't know. I blocked most of the stuff out from my childhood. There was something that happened really bad when I was a kid…it's the type of thing that you don't want to ever happen to a kid….It was like completely crossing boundaries…there was a point where I wanted to find him (participant's father) and obliterate him. I wanted to find a way to blow him up into pieces because he was not there to protect me from this other man. I can remember being so angry and I can remember what the pain felt like. I was so pissed that he wasn't there. I would clinch my fist and people could see the anger I had towards my dad."

Robert: "It was messed up for a little kid, at a young age. I started doing a lot of wrong (Participant laughs); for my dad and with my dad. As a little kid I never shit…what do I say…I was grown up quick bro, I learned things quick. Yea, I had to take care of myself. I didn't like it but…I had to deal with it…I was pissed off. He would miss my games and shit like that."

Steve: "As a child I was on my own. My mom worked three jobs and I was always alone. It was an interesting way of being; I mean being on your own all the time with no adults. I grew up real quick. In high school I worked more. I wish I could go back and had the opportunity to pursue my dreams instead of having to grow up so fast because I had no adults in my life. I would have had that pressure of having to find a job because I have to help pay rent. I could have gone back to school and done anything. Growing up I would hear my friends talk about their dad and how their dads would do things with them and teach them how to ride a bike or skateboard. I didn't have all that. So for me it was like ok, that's cool, whatever. I would bug my mom for these things but I knew she couldn't and I didn't have time for those things because I had to work…When you grow up in a home without a father you don't have a male figure to attach to. So you are going to look for something else to attach to, it could be good or bad, but you will find something to attach to."

Theme Four: Talking about Absent Father

During the interview, participants were asked to share their en vivo experience discussing their father. They were asked, "How does it feel to talk about you father." Some participants enjoyed discussing their father, however, one was indifferent and one became angry and upset. Although each participant shared the same variable (absent father), talking about him was experienced in different ways.

Jonathan:    "It feels good to talk about my dad. I never really talked about it. I never got this deep. I never do this with anyone. I was uncomfortable talking to other people about this kind of stuff. I used to feel uncomfortable talking about my father. But now I am able to talk about him."

Robert:    "This shit is pissing me off talking about this shit. I don't like talking about the shit he has done, but I like talking about him and remembering him."

Steve:    "I am comfortable talking about my dad. It feels good to talk about my dad. I have to let it off my shoulders. Years ago I was angry about it and did not want to bring it up, but now I realize that I have to talk about it, or I am going to live with all this anger."

Ruben:    It is fun to talk about my father. I feel good, I have accepted the situation. I have accepted him and appreciate him as well as the situation. I was given the opportunity to stop the cycle. To improve the males who have the same last name as me."

Theme Five: Experiences in School

A common theme emerged surrounding participants' experience and behaviors in school. During their childhood, individuals showed disruptive behaviors and problems with academic performance. Each participant noted their experience in school was somewhat related to their father's absence.

Steve:    "School was fun, yet it was entertaining for me. Watching people grow. They would always talk about their family. They would always talk about their dads and their family. I was very observant of people when they would talk about their family and their dad."

Mike:    "I had to deal with his absence because it fucked with me as a child and as an adult. When I got to college I had to deal with feelings of being inept. I used to feel like I wasn't good enough to be at college. I used to see my behavior, bickering with my coaches and other students as a reflection of inadequacy stemming from my father being gone. If my dad was around he would have helped me through these times when I didn't know who I was. I would do great on my tests and I would understand all the information in school, but there was this constant nag in my head that told me I didn't belong there and I was inadequate. But around my junior year I started to figure it out and tell myself that I can make it."

Theme Six: Significant Adults who were Supportive

The role of father was left vacant in each of these participants' lives, consequently, they found a significant adult who was supportive and provided guidance. Searching and finding a role model was a theme which emerged as the participants discussed their experience without a father.

Jonathan:     "My mother and my uncles played a role in my life; also my aunt and my grandmother. My uncles played a father role in my life. They would discipline me and put that fear in my heart. My uncle would keep me in check, he was the disciplinarian. My uncle would always be right there."

Robert:     "My uncle, He was my mom's brother. He was like my dad too growing up. When I was a kid, like nine years old, that's when I learned how to drive bro. I taught myself how to drive. Even if my dad was in or out, I would drive over there (his uncle's house). Any chance I got I would go to my uncle's house."

Steve:        "Around age 12 I had my best friends dad who was kind of a father figure, he would give words of advice…. I also felt very curious about my father. But my mom would fill that void. She would take me to sign up for baseball and karate. She made sure I had what the other kids had, except for a father figure."

Ruben:      "My girlfriend's father has become a positive role model for me. I have become close with him over time."

Ravon      "My Uncles, aunts played a large role in my childhood. I talked to them every day."

Mike:        "There was this one boyfriend of my mom who was around from age 6 to age 9. He was the one male ventral role model in my life. He was the longest most prolific male in my life and he only lasted 3 years."

Category Two: Perceptions of Paternal Absence

The following four subthemes within this category emerged from the interviews.

<u>Theme Seven: Significant Memories of Father</u>

Participant's presented memories of their father which mirrored the way they felt about him. If a participant presented as neutral towards his father he had no memory of him, if he had a pleasant memory then his feelings were more positive, and the recollection of a painful memory resembled aversive feelings towards the father.

Jonathan:    "My father left when I was ten. I only saw my father 1 time in my life. I remember the day. He came in the morning and my mom was like your father is here. He would always promise to come but he never did. Then one day my mother was like "your father is here, and I ran and hugged him. It was exciting for the first time to see him. He stood around for like 2-3 days and I probably spoke to him 3 times after that. It felt like Christmas seeing him. I was super surprised when he came. When he didn't come I wasn't depressed or surprised, I just expected him to disappoint me. It wasn't anything to depressing. I really stopped caring and I started to say I will believe it when I see it. However, That first day I say him we didn't do anything special. I was just by his side all day. We just walked through the neighborhood all day. I don't really have any other memories of him."

Willy:      "I have no memories of my father. He was gone 26 out of the 28 years of my life."

Robert:      "The bad memory was…. always going with him and stealing and shit. At the same time I was a little kid and knew what he was doing. I hated it, but back then I knew I was going to get broken off with some money. He would bribe me. Just that shit, that's a bad memory, you know, seeing him overdosing and shit, him getting arrested and shit. No kid should see shit like that, lot of bad but a lot of good too. Another memory was when I was little, we were at some party and there was some dude, younger than my dad just started talking shit. He was on him all day. Since I was there my dad really didn't do anything. So my dad told me to take a walk and go down the street. He was calling him punk bitch, fucking punk bitch. I heard all this going on and I was a little kid. I knew what was going to happen already and I was scared as fuck. My dad whooped the shit out of him. I told my dad, "What happened? Why did you do that? What's a punk?" He told me, "Don't let anyone ever call you a punk." So I took that to the heart, because my dad told me, you know. It could have been good or bad, but since my dad told me, I took it to heart. Shit, growing up, I just hated when people would call me a punk."

Steve:     "When I was 11 years old I found out I had a father. Growing all the way up to 11 years old I thought my father was gone, dead. They told me he was dead. But when I was 11 someone pointed him out to me. Some said, "Hey look, that's your dad." When they showed me my father I did not believe it. I cried and ran out of the restaurant. It was a shock."

Mike:      "When I was playing football at USC, I used to see guys on the team and their father's would stay with them after practice and help work on their technique. I remember watching those situations and think, "Damn, it would have been nice to let my father be there to see his son on the team." I felt sad for him, because he could have enjoyed this with me."

Theme Eight: Changes in Perceptions and Feelings

Subtheme eight was a major finding in the research. Participants discussed their feelings towards their father and how they have changed over time. As children, adolescents, and adults, participants noted feeling different towards their father's associated with their thoughts surrounding his absence. The continuum of experiences began with confusion, anger, and loneliness; with conscious effort, they moved to acceptance, understanding, and even love. Becoming parents was also a variable which moved participants into an empathetic position, consequently changing the way they felt towards their father. This theme highlights the fluidity and flexibility of feelings and perception.

Jonathan: "Overtime I got smarter, more mature, and more understanding of what is going on and why he left. My other brothers and sisters never had their fathers, so no one was going to feel sorry for me. They didn't have their fathers either. I let go of a lot of this stuff. That just me. My perception has changed a little bit form when I was a kid; putting all the information together. As a kid, he tried one time. I kept talking till him a little bit and was curious about him.. He was trying when I was a kid, and me being that age I am going to accept him at least trying. Now its just different. If he called me today, I would be like, "I live over her call me if you want to come and I will meet you at the airport." I wouldn't be all excited. As a child I wasn't chasing him but I was looking, expecting, desiring, wanting to see him. He was calling me. I wanted him to come around but I didn't try to go where he was at. I wanted him to come where I was at. I still want him to come, if I found information to get in touch with him."

Willy: "My son has impacted the way I feel about my dad. Having my son helped me realize how the father son relationship would be. He has made me realize how much I want my father. My relationship with my son…him wanting to be with me and wanting to play with me…makes me want to be with my father more. I have never felt being wanted the way my son wants me. My son wants me so bad. I used to look for that feeling in girls. I used to search for that so hard. That love. Now I kind of hate them now and realize I don't need them anymore. I got what I need in my son."

Robert:      "My son has helped change my feelings towards my father. Before my son I was always pissed off, more anger. But after my son, I guess he taught me to love my dad more."

Steve:      "I got over the anger towards this guy. I met him one more time 2 years ago and all the rage was gone. There was no point to it. He is not angry over me so why should I be angry over him… Ever since I met my wife and got back into church I don't hate my father as much. I don't have the anger or resentment towards him anymore."

Eloy:      "The biggest thing that has impacted the way I feel about my father is the letters that I stumbled upon. I was astonished that my dad touched this piece of paper. He is not just some mythical guy out there but he is a human being. That was a turning point where my feelings sort of changed. This was just a year ago."

Theme Nine: Current Perception of Father's Absence

Participants had different understandings of where there fathers were and why they were not in the home. Subtheme nine demonstrated that paternal absence can be understood and experienced in many ways. Although they all grew up without a father, their perception of his absence varies.

Willy:      "He couldn't take it. It wasn't just him, my mom left him too. He thought, "if I stay here I'm stuck." I guess he didn't want to be stuck with me."

Robert:      "My dad was gone because he was a drug addict. My dad was always a drug addict but he always had a job you know? But at the same time, being a drug addict and having a family and rent, and everything he had to do."

Steve:    "My dad had a wife and another family on the side. Many men have mistresses, turns out my mom happened to be the mistress."

Ruben:    "As I get to know more and more about my father, I start to understand that he had to be the way he was because he was raised in tough conditions. His life wasn't easy so I understand his way if being. My father did not know any better. This is not what people have told me but it is my reasoning, my own rationalization. For example, when it rains, some people would explain it as God is crying. Is God crying? No! But the reasoning makes people feel better and allows them to live with a situation they do not understand. It's the reasoning that has helped me."

Ravon:    "Why was my father absent in my life? That, I have no idea. Besides the fact that my mom said he was kind of selfish, and my mom told me that he already had a kid. But the real reason, I don't know. He never gave us the real reason why he left."

Mike:     "Ultimately, I feel my father was absent in my life because of his socioeconomic status. He was a victim of his environment. He made multiple decisions that ruined his life. The final case was the one that put him away. (Participant reluctantly continues), the final charge was violence related with a fire arm. I feel like this is fucked up but ultimately, I came out ok and had a great mom. I was not the only one who went through it. Millions of guys go through not having a dad. I feel blessed that at least my mom was there but I feel sad that society creates these situations without it being necessary. I feel a character flaw developed because of my father's environment…I would explain my dad as lost and confused. He was barely a kid, he couldn't raise a kid. He was a young kid who needed a father himself. He made a mistake; he shouldn't have had me that young."

Paul: "I consider my father being absent even when he was in my life. But I believe he was absent because he was not a supportive father. He never truly (long pause) was committed to his wife, my mother, he was never committed to us as children. I don't think he loved he. He was never committed; he never wanted to buy a house that is why we rented. If you buy a house that is commitment and he never wanted to do that with us. When he left us he got with another woman who had two kids, he took care of those kids when he had his own. He did not take care of us but he took care of someone who wasn't his blood."

Eloy: "My father chose not to be in my life. That's why he was absent. If you really care about something you will be there, bottom line; that is not an excuse. His cultural issues are valid but it is not an excuse for leaving his son. If he really wanted to be a part of my life he would be. It is difficult for me to answer that because I can't read his mind. But I am somewhat able to understand his mind."

Theme Ten: Acquired Values Related to Absent Father

Subtheme ten highlights the specific values that each participant has acquired surrounding their experience without a father.

Jonathan: "I am a good person, I am not the best father but I will try. I value family and friends. I value being a good father. I know how it is. I have two other sons in different states. He comes out here to visit me sometimes. And my cousin… I mean my son, I still talk to his mother all the time. I'm just like my father how he did to me and my mother. But times are different now. His absence did influence me but in a small role but not that much. Him not being there has not made me want to work extra hard to be around my kids because I am not working extra hard to see them. He hasn't really affected me to be a better father to my kids. I am here with my daughter right now and her mother and I am going to make the most out of this time."

Robert:    "The only thing in my life that I value is my son. I have learned that a good dad is one who is around his son all the time, raising him, being with his son. I want to show him the ropes of life. The good ones you know… good values. Shit, it's not cool! (Participant laughs). Not having a dad…umm what can I say, every son needs a dad, the way I see it. Like I would not go to my mom for certain things, shit I needed to talk about and get off my chest. Every boy needs a dad."

Mike:    "Fatherlessness…(long pause) means discarded. That's the first word that comes to my mind. When you are fatherless, it is like someone didn't care for you, didn't think enough of you and you are discarded. Its one thing if your dad died or was gone for a legitimate cause, but it says something when he can be there and you are still fatherless. I felt thrown away like a McDonald's cup. However, if you grow up without a father; you can still grow up alright. A lot of people have excuses and blame it on their father being gone, but if you have one solid parent you are doing a lot better than many other people."

Paul: "Your dad leaving really changes your life. It puts your life on a whole different path. I had to pick up his slack and I think it makes it hard on everyone when the father leaves."

Category Three: Feelings towards Father

The following five subthemes within this category emerged from the interviews.

<u>Theme Eleven: Dynamics of Current Feelings towards Father</u>

Subthemes eleven is divided into two sections; a) classification of feelings, and b) management of feelings. a) Each participant explained their current feelings towards their father. The range of feelings is classified as either; negative, neutral, or positive. Some participants had both positive and negative feelings towards which is classified as, "combined" feelings towards father. b) Participants management of their emotions was classified as displacement or processing, which is working through one's feelings.

Jonathan: a) <u>Neutral</u> "I don't have any feelings towards my father. Time heals all things. I am 33 years old and time heals all. It has been 23 years of time past since I last spoke to him so I have no current feelings towards him. Time has healed any anger towards him. I would be excited to see him but if I don't I don't really care. It's been twenty-three years, one more day is not going to hurt."

Willy: <u>Negative</u> "I told him if he ever sees me on the street cross the street because I will beat you up. I told him that I want him to be different so instead of wanting to beat him up, I go hug him and love him. But sometimes I think, "No dad, I made it this far. I'll do the same without you. I'm a fucking phoenix, you don't know me... In time my struggles will kill me but I'll rise from the ashes or fade from memory doing my best. I'm going to prove you wrong, wait for the confirmation to hit your ears from others because I am mute to you as well as deaf. I'm going to a do shit... I'm going to fucking do shit with my life!"

Steve:     Negative "I did not even know that my father lived in the same neighborhood as me. That means when I was on the bus on the way to school, I could have been next to him. I could have bumped shoulders with this man and never even know. I found it fucked up. What an asshole. Now I find it hilarious though. I could have bumped into him so many times….As a child you hear a dad is supposed to do certain things for you, growing up to be a man, growing up to learn about life. You know, teaching you morals, teaching you boundaries. The resentment of looking like him comes from all that."

Ravon:     Neutral "I don't have any resentment or anything. I never knew any fathers so it was just normal not having a dad. There was never any anger or any resentment. I would just wonder and be curious mostly. I'm going off of TV. I would see people on shows having moms and dads and I would, I guess, I would wonder how that would feel. I was curious how it would feel to have a dad."

Mike:     Positive: "Honestly, being a grown man, I really have no ill will towards my dad. My mom explained it to me which made me feel better. My dad grew up in a home where his mom would drink and smoke weed with him. His mom would give him the drug supply to go sell at school to his friends. I am big on taking everything into account, and that is just what he knew. My mom told me that before he started taking drugs, he was a good father. He took care of me and she showed me pictures as a baby where I was asleep on his chest. He was cool. He just had a problem when he started crack and cocaine. I really am able to understand he was not able to cope. This helped me to understand that it is not good to avoid your problems. I have learned to address problems and take them head on. I saw my father as trying to run away from an issue. Everybody has their crutch, but I learned to address my problems…However, when I think about my father, feelings of disappointment and regret come up; disappointment because he failed me when I was a child, him being addicted to drugs. I realized he had a character issue. He would sober up in jail and when he would get out he would immediately return to using and not come to see his kid. That to me is a character issue. He would be out of jail, start using drugs again, then in 2 weeks be right back in jail."

Ruben:   b) Displacement "My father smoked cigarettes heavily and drank heavily. I hate cigarettes so much because of this reason. He would have yellow fingernails, dry skin, and that smell. When I smell cigarettes I think of my father. I would be very angry if my son started to smoke. I have smoked cigar, but the first time I did it in Miami I just did not feel comfortable. One thing I will not put up with in my life is family members smoking cigarettes; it's just my decision. Smoking is a trigger for me. When I smell cigarettes, I get triggered and all the resentment and bad memories come up."

Eloy:   Displacement "I have never really thought about my feelings towards my father. I really just used to blame my mother and be frustrated towards her. As I became a teenager, I started to feel that anger and resentment facilitated by not having a dad. I would direct some of that anger to my mom and I would think, "It is your fault (mom) that we are in this situation."

Mike:  Processing "My father had a son (participant referring to himself) who was an over achiever, I feel sad that he did not get to experience me. If I was a dad I would have loved to see a kid like me grow up and become who I am today. If he could have done it all over, he would have changed it. I don't feel anger towards him, I just feel sad that he made those decisions to ruin his life. I have thought about this and him for a long time. I had to figure it out.

Theme Twelve: Current Desire for One's Father

Participants described their desire for a father. Some had had no desire while others wanted their father in their lives.

Jonathan:  "If he came back into my life, I would feel another chapter would be opened. I don't know if I would call it closure but I would look at him and ask, where you been? I would want him to come back in my life."

Willy:  "I want an attempt at reconciliation with my father. I learned that shit is trivial...everything get better with time."

Steve:  "I would not let him in my life. I would not give him my number, email, address, I wouldn't give him anything. I wouldn't give him that pleasure...I don't want to go where I thought I was going as a child. It wasn't so much of a depression it was more being rebellious. I was wild. However, doing what I was doing help me, it helped me grow. When I have kids, there will be no way in hell that I will let them be like I was as a child. So that makes me a better person. I don't want that fool to put his two cents in mine."

Ruben:     "When my dad left as a child it was empowering, when he died and I was an adult it was frustrating. I wanted to connect with him and start a new relationship but I was unable to. It was frustrating because I wanted to take control of a situation, but I couldn't."

Ravon:     "I don't necessarily want him back in my life, I just want to know why he left? f I could talk to my dad I would want to ask him what's the point? Because I knew he had kids with other women and I would like to ask him what is the point of abandoning his kids and why would he abandon all three of us?"

Paul:     "I am adult now, so, him coming back into my life wouldn't affect me. I am set in my path. However, I wouldn't let him be a part of my life. I wouldn't confide in him and I wouldn't search him out."

## Theme Thirteen: Feelings Regarding Father's Absence

Subtheme thirteen is a description of the participants' feelings towards the reason their father was absent. This major finding also shows the various effects these feelings have had on the participants.

Jonathan:     "I wanted to know why he wasn't there. Maybe he didn't live in New York, I don't know. I do want to know the reason why he wasn't around. It doesn't really bother me though."

Mike: "My father being in jail really fucked with my mind (Participant then presented with delayed speech, and proceeded to put his head down. Participant had difficulty discussing his father in jail). I felt like it made me want to always watch my actions because I could end up there…It was not like my dad was a fool. My dad was a very successful drug dealer. At least these Columbians and mobsters put some money away for their families. My dad didn't do that. He went and blew all of his money and left nothing for his wife and kid. My feelings towards my father were neutral because I understand his life as a child and he had a tough situation growing up. But as a man you have to take responsibility for your actions. So now it is negative, I have a negative opinion towards him."

Paul: "Regarding my father's absence…I think it is weak. He was a conformist. He was content with the basic things in life. I am the opposite. I have a negative perception to his lack of commitment. However, he was disciplined and a hard worker, much like me. How do I feel about his death? I wouldn't wish death upon anyone and I am not happy that he is dead. But that is life, I am not broken up about it. I am pretty neutral about his death. Indifferent you could say."

Eloy: "I am somewhat neutral on my feelings towards him. I think it is unfortunate that my father wasn't able to make up his own mind about choosing who he can have a family with. I do feel hurt about this reason but I have come to accept it and deal with it. It pissed me off at first but I have come to be more empathetic towards him. Towards his culture, I am frustrated. I have this feeling of being powerless, and I can't change the Indian culture but I want my dad. I have conflicting feelings, my whole life I have grown up not liking my father but as I have gotten older, I have learned to adopt the philosophy that shit happens for a reason. I would not want anything to change. I don't know who I would be or where I would be if he was around so I am appreciative of the person I have become."

## Theme Fourteen: Childhood Feelings towards Father

Participants presented descriptions of childhood feelings towards their father. Some of these feelings have changed while others have stayed the same.

Jonathan: "Sometimes I wanted to see him I wanted to know who he was. I wanted to see what kind of person he was. I had a desire to meet him...I don't know how I felt when I was little. I just went on with my life. My other never really talked about him. My aunts always asked about him and I gave them the same answer, I don't know where my father is. I guess I was frustrated. I never had anyone who understood me or got me. Most of my friends had their fathers and they could go see them. I felt no one understood me."

Willy: "It was rage! I had rage towards my father!"

Robert: "I would try to act like I didn't care you know. It would bother me. I was just pissed off bro! You know. At the same time I knew he had to do what he had to do, but...I was still pissed."

Steve: "There was a lot of resentment for him. It was all because I didn't have my dad. I would often get depressed, I had a dad who was alive but I didn't have one physically next to me."

Ravon:      "Curiosity played a role in my life when I was younger. I didn't know how to feel so I was just curious about him, who he was, where he was, and just him as a human."

Mike:      "As a kid I had more of a "fuck you" personality towards my father. The fact that he wasn't there wasn't the problem with me. The fact was that when he was in jail he would write me and promise that we were going to spend time together. But when he would get out he would leave me sitting there, not call and not show up.

Eloy:      "As a child I had conflicting feelings towards my mother, at times she was my world and other times I found myself frustrated and annoyed with her. As a kid I was confused, I did not understand why I was the only kid without a father.

Theme Fifteen: Connecting with Absent Father

Participants were asked, "If you could contact your father would you?" Minor theme 5 is a description of participants' desire, or lack thereof, to connect with their absent father.

Jonathan:      "Yes, I would like to just find out information about him. How old is he, is he married, where does he live? It wouldn't be any anger or frustration. I am past the angry point you could basically say. The angry point was at the beginning when I was a child. When he would keep disappointing me and never show up. I wasn't in my teens more like when I was ten years old."

Willy:      "If my dad were to come back into my life I would eat that day up, like if it was a buffet. I have been waiting for that for so many years. Just for him to realize his mistakes and say I am sorry. I want him to try to make it right. I could be 60 and him to come in my life and from that day on try to make it better, I just want my dad."

Steve:  "Currently I just want to talk to him. I actually told my wife, because of my religion I want to talk to him and give him the benefit of the doubt. I have to go in there with an open mind and an open heart, because if he says something about my mom I can't hit him. The possibility of losing my job is too great and I would not lose it because of him. In the past the possibility of swinging on my father if I saw him was huge; but not anymore…If I were to contact him I would want to know why my father offered my mom money to get rid of me when she was pregnant with me. This is what I am angry about. This is what started all my anger towards him."

Ruben:  "If my dad came back into my life I would definitely want to sit down with him and talk. But I wouldn't ask him questions about why he left and our past. I would catch him up with my life and tell him about his grandson. I would not want him to be my father but more be the grandfather to my son. I think since I have accepted his absence and understood it; I am better equipped to cope with it."

Mike:  "I thought about going to see my father in jail, but at this point I would be indifferent to him. I know he is my dad, but I have got this far without him. He has not had any effect or imprinting anything on my life; whatsoever, on anything I have done. I would let me dad have my phone number, but I don't see how he would be a part of my life. I would not take the effort to allow him back into my life. That would take away the focus on what I am trying to accomplish."

Paul:        "If I could talk to him I would. I wouldn't confront him or anything."

Eloy:        "No I am not really interested in contacting my father. I would not really be interested in what he is doing. If I were to run into him, I wouldn't want to ruin his family."

Category Four: Coping without a Father

The following six subthemes within this category emerged from the interviews.

<u>Theme Sixteen: Childhood Behaviors</u>

Subtheme sixteen describes participants' childhood behaviors in the absence of their father. All of the participants expressed that the way they felt about their father was a factor that motivated their behaviors.

Jonathan:    "Growing up in New York City you automatically hang out with a lot of people. I did what most of the people did around me. I had millions of friends; drug dealer friends, athletic sports friends, a bunch of different friends. I never sold drugs."

Willy:      "As I grew up without a father I had to look happy all the time because people start questioning you when you are sad. I would wake up some days and say to myself "today is going to be a shitty day." I'm tired of hearing about your perfect life and your cookie cutter life…your whole Andy Griffith show bull shit…I know you have a perfect life and my life is fucked up."

Eloy:        "As a kid I had times where I would act out and get aggressive. But usually it was just towards my mom…if my dad would have been around I think I would have acted different, but sine he wasn't there I was like I can do whatever I want, because he is not going to do anything."

Robert: "I never was a bad kid, but I tried to be always on the street, never wanted to be inside. Yea, when he was gone I would act a fool you know, out of anger but I could also do what I wanted to do. But like when he was out, he straightened me out. But now, I am a fucking grown man, but I still need my dad to tell me shit, that's what I don't got right now."

Steve: "Before I knew my dad was alive I behaved like a regular child; do my homework, play around, clean the house. I had rules. After I found out my dad was alive I started to wild out a little but... I became rebellious.

Ruben: "Before my father left I was a normal kid when my dad was around. I knew I had the potential to be whatever I wanted to in life. I used to be very laid back. School came easy to me. But when my dad left I took the responsible role when my dad left. At 11 years old I did really well in school and I started getting really focused. My brother dealt with it one way and I dealt with it in another way. At this time my mom used to cry herself to sleep. I would go and lay with her and hold her and tell her it was going to be fine. I would wait till she fell asleep then I would feel comfortable enough to fall asleep. I was comforting my mom."

Ravon: "I was pretty good kid. I never really got in trouble and it wasn't really that serious."

Mike:      "I had a gradual progression. I used to get into so many fights; I used to have a huge temper. Any person who would say anything to me that was offensive, I would punch them."

Theme Seventeen: Perceived Effects Related to Father's Absence: Motivation

Participants described paternal absence to have certain effects on their lives. Some of these effects are perceived as detrimental, while others have had a more positive effect on the participants' lives. Using their father's absence as motivation is another factor which is presented in subtheme seventeen.

Robert:    "I have learned to just be a cut throat kind of guy because my dad was gone. I learned that I needed to take care myself however I can and to forget everyone else. I was angry at him and I found that I took my anger out on him onto other people but I am learning how to deal with my feelings and know that even though my dad was in jail it is possible that he is still a good man and loved me...when he died I found myself not as angry at him like I was when he was in jail"

Steve:     "I can't be emotional with another man when he talks about kids or fathers because I never had that. Also, if my dad was around I would have been more motivated. But overtime his absence became a motivation for me to better myself...Him being gone makes me want to be an amazing father. I am going to be there and make sure that I did everything he didn't do for me. Now that I am married I have to make sure I am not him at all. I reference all my negativity towards him. I don't want to be anything like him, I don't want any part of him in my life."

Paul: "I am the man who I am today because of all the experiences I have gone through. I faced all those things and overcome all of those obstacles much like a domino effect. Because of his initial action, I have become the man I am."

Eloy: "I see my father as any other dude. That has one thing that has motivated me to be so career driven, family oriented and all about success, because I don't want to be just any other dude. I don't want to be like him."

Willy: "When my son says, "I love you daddy," that would trigger the fuck out of me! I would not be able to hear someone say I love you like that. I even had my girlfriend just say she cares about me but don't say I love you. In regards to relationships with other people, I have never heard anyone say.. "you are a fucking ass hole I don't want to talk to you." Its always been the opposite. You look like a build scary wilder beast, then we get to talk to you and hear your views and you are a delightful person. All you think about is other people and you never put yourself first. People know I am can be a violent person, but they tend to know that I am a much deeper person and I am able to feel for other people and make sure they know that they are understood."

## Theme Eighteen: Feelings of Self: Maladaptive Cycle and Avoiding Self Hatred

Participants described feelings and perceptions of themselves. Two variables emerged in this theme a) Maladaptive Cycle and b) Avoiding Self Hatred. These two variables highlight how paternal absence affects the way individuals view themselves.

Ruben: Maladaptive Cycle "I think I am a father that is struggling to live up to his own expectations; I want to be a father who is working to improve himself and his family…I was absent for a year and a half from my son's life. I was a coward back then. I did not want to be a father and was in denial. I had to make a conscious effort to be in denial. I would drive to her house and wait outside week after week and never go knock on the door. I would want to just leave the bull shit and be the father I know I can be. I had another relationship and we were talking about having kids. But I already had a kid and I saw myself becoming my father. I was continuing the cycle, I told myself this is something that I would never do but her I was doing it. So I had to make an effort to change. When I made the decision to step up and be a father it was because of my dad. I was mad at myself because in some ways I became him. If I would have gone with what was easy I would have become my father. But I realized I was not him, so I came back home to my son and his mother. I was scared to be like my father, I was scared that I was going to fail as a father. I was scared that I was not going to stop the cycle and I was not going to be good enough; that's partly why I was not around. I still carry that fear but I constantly have to challenge it."

Ravon: Maladaptive Cycle "One thing I did learn about him and about him leaving us is that his father did the same thing to him. It was like a cycle. I sometimes worry that I'm going to do the same thing but I'm not really trying to have kids right now."

Mike:     Maladaptive Cycle "My dad fell into the footsteps of his dad. My grandfather was a lot like the way my dad was. I don't want to be like that and I don't want to continue that cycle."

Paul:     Avoiding Self Hatred "My father was a hardworking and complaisant and selfish individual. He was complacent with what he had. No ambitions to better himself. I am totally the opposite; I am always striving to succeed and to better myself and my family."

Eloy:     Avoiding Self Hatred "I see my father as any other dude. That has one thing that has motivated me to be so career driven, family oriented and all about success, because I don't want to be just any other dude. I don't want to be like him."

Steve:    Avoiding Self Hatred "I am so glad in life that I don't look like him. I would have resented myself if I did look like him. The resentment comes from him not being around and not being a father.

Theme Nineteen: Parenting: The Importance of Paternal Modeling

Participants were asked, "Do you want to be a parent?" Each participant answered their feelings regarding parenting and the importance of having a father.

Researcher:   "Can you describe your idea of a father, in general?"

Ravon    "Honestly, I can't even answer that question. I don't know what a father is. I guess an absent father is a bad father. Honestly I can't even describe what a good or bad father is because any of the people I have ever hung around with; none of them had close fathers. It was a big group of people without fathers...I wouldn't mind being a parent but I am sure it would take some kind of practice...I think I would make a decent parent. I would learn from my father's mistakes and not make the same ones with my kids. Honestly I have no idea what makes a great parent. Like I would want someone to rate me on my parenting because I don't know what it is. And the Same thing applies to a bad parent. I can't even tell you what a bad parent is, it is like a huge part of what I should have been taught about being a man and a father from my dad is missing."

Mike:  "I don't know what a good father is, from what I have seen so far, basically is someone who is there…someone who tries to do right by their kids. Overall, a good dad is someone who was there who had your back. I really don't know but I guess a bad father is someone who is there but who makes the choice not to be there. Someone who can be there for their kid but actively chooses not to, that is a bad father to me. But yea, I want to be a parent. I think I will be a good dad. I think I will be very involved but somewhat reserved. I will let me kid to figure out their own personality, their likes and dislikes."

Theme Twenty: What makes a Family

Participants gave a description of their current family and their views on what makes a family.

Ruben:  "My immediate family is a combination of craziness and fun. My extended family, they are good. I have a supportive family. My brother is sometimes nonexistent when it comes to helping with my mom, but hey, it is what it is."

Ravon:  "I have a dysfunctional family. Besides my immediate family, my mother and my grandmother are considered my family."

Mike:        "Family are people who care for my wellbeing and I care for theirs. My family is my mom. It is just her and I growing up. I was raised by my grandmother and 4 aunts. I was raised by all women. My family is my mom. Family are people who care for my wellbeing and I care for theirs."

Paul:        "I have a mother and two younger brothers. My mother is a hard working mother…I have two younger brothers who both have children. I consider friends and blood to be family."

Eloy:        "I only know my mom's side of the family. Were close but we are not super close. But I consider family whoever you have a close strong relationship too. It could be family but it also could be friends."

Theme Twenty-One: Father's Day

Participants described their experience on Father's Day. They described how they feel and what they do during the time when people celebrate fathers.

Ruben:        "I miss him during Father's Day. I get emotional thinking that there is a potential to fail my son. So I start to become worried. I think as long as my son does not have the void that I felt towards my father, and then I feel I would be successful as a father. I want my son to recognize that I was there for me."

Steve:        "When Father's Day comes around I always look for a father who I can go celebrate with. I am going to enjoy myself and not be miserable. He probably doesn't think about me, so why should I think about him."

Ravon:        "On Father's Day I don't even think about my father; for what?"

Mike:        "I usually do something with my mom on Father's Day. I get her double gifts because she was like mom and dad rolled into one."

Paul: "I thought about my father on father's day and wanted to visit him at the cemetery but I did not go. On Father's Day I want to spotlight my brothers who are fathers now. I celebrate them because they are fathers; instead of festering in thoughts of my dad."

Eloy: "Father's Day is usually treated as "Single Mother's Day" for me."

Theme Twenty-Two: Understanding the Male Role

Throughout their experience, participants developed an idea of what a man is, how he should act, and representations of the male role. They described how their experience without a father has impacted their perceptions of men.

Jonathan: "A man is someone who has a lot of responsibilities and takes care of those responsibilities. A man who is there for people. My father did not fit that role as a man when I was ten but now maybe he does. I am starting to ease into that role as a man."

Willy: "A man can only be judged by the solidity of his word…a person who does not stand by their word and breaks their promises is a coward. A man works for his family. If I make a promise to my son I will go through hell to keep it."

Robert: "I know I am a man bro, but sometimes I feel like a kid still. And I trip out too because, I feel like I didn't….I don't want to use it as an excuse but I feel I was grown so quick. I mean fuck, I didn't have time to be a kid."

Steve: "When do you become a man, is it when you first have sex, when you make your first dollar, no! You have to grow into a man and become a man. Being a man you have to own up to your own responsibilities. No one can make you into a man, you have to earn it for yourself... A man is someone who owns up to their responsibilities."

Ruben: "A man is a provider and protector."

Ravon: "All the men in my life were not really men, at least I wouldn't consider them that. My idea of a man is kind of blank."

Mike: "A man is somebody who deals with his shit. Men handle their problems head on. If I had to describe it in one word, I would say a man is accountable."

Paul: "A man is someone who works hard and takes care of business. No bull shit and faces obstacles head on. An example of this is one day when my father physically protected me. I remember as a kid I was 8 or 9 years old walking into a pet store. Some guy was walking out and just threw the door and it hit me. My dad told the guy that he needs to be careful and the man said, "No your son needs to be careful." So my dad beat his ass. I'm glad that he protected me. I feel like that is a good example of a man."

## Chapter V

### Discussion

The current study sought to develop research regarding the experience of individuals who grew up without their fathers. Their feelings towards and perceptions of the participants absent fathers were highlighted as the study's forefront interest; how have they developed and what role do they currently play in the individual's lives. This study was developed using a phenomenological approach that closely followed the work of Giorgi (1985). In addition, other theorists who were followed included Patton (1990) and Creswell (1994). This chapter contains findings from the research in the following four categories: The Experience without a Father, Perceptions of Paternal Absence, Coping without a Father, Feelings towards Father.

### General Findings

The purpose of this research was to gain a better understanding of how individuals' perception of and feelings towards their absent father play a role in their lives. Nine male participants were interviewed and asked to disclose their experiences growing up without a father. These individuals highlighted their external worlds as well as their internal experiences which were related to one another. Individuals' internal experiences were affected by their environments; conversely, the environment was also influenced by the individual's internal process. Some of the findings in this study were similar to those previously done by researchers examining paternal absence; parentification (Knox, Zusman, & DeCuzzi, 2004), acting out behaviors (Santrock 1977, Montare, 1980), adopting paternal figures (Mulkey, Crain, & Hamington, 1992).

**The Experience without a Father**

The first category The Experience without a Father is comprised of six subthemes. These themes include: *1) Relationships with Mother, 2) Discussions about Absent Father, 3) Childhood Experience without a Father: Parentification and Defenses, 4) Talking about Absent Father, 5) Experiences in School,* and *6) Significant Adults who were Supportive.* The findings in this category showed various experiences with a similar variable; an absent father. The findings showed how individuals can experience the same event yet internalize it, perceive it, and react to it, in different ways.

The individuals in this study discussed the relationship with their mothers; their experience of paternal absence allowed for a stronger bond to be formed with the remaining parent. However, the individuals also reported, at times, challenges with their mother. As experienced by the participants, the absence of a father tends to alter an individual's view of their mother and the mother-son relationship. Some of the participants were able to discuss their father with their mother, however others were not. The ability to talk about one's absent father is an important characteristic of growing up without him in the home. The discussions within the family allow an individual to create a standing perception of the father as well as an understanding of his absence. An inability to discuss one's absent father facilitates ambiguity and confusion within a child, thus, it is important to have open discussions that give insight into the situation.

Much like the findings in Knox, Zusman, & DeCuzzi's (2004) research, participants discussed becoming parentified and taking on responsibilities of a parent. For example, participants disclosed having to find jobs to supplement income for the family; they also discussed becoming the source of emotional support and security for their mother's. Being parentified is a seemingly universal experience for these participants.

Another shared experience found in this research is the use of psychological defenses to manage feelings brought about by an absent father. As a child, some participants rationalized their absent father as a normal part of growing up, while others denied anger and aversive feelings towards him. Currently, participants explained repressing childhood memories in order to alleviate pain cause by unwanted thoughts. The use of defenses to protect ego functioning, whatever they may be, is a phenomenon that occurs when an individual is raised without a father.

In order to identify aspects surrounding the process of talking about one's absent father, the participants were asked to disclose the experience in vivo. Some of the participants felt no physical or emotional sensations while others became distraught and needed to take a break from the interviews. The individuals who felt little sensatory stimuli tended to have positive or neutral feelings/perceptions of their absent father. Those who experienced aversive internal processes maintained a negative view of the paternal absence. This observed experience indicates a connection between one's perception of another and their physical/emotional experiences.

This concept is highlighted in Ellis's (1995) theory of REBT; a person's experience has nothing to do with the event itself, rather, the individual's perceptions and beliefs of the experience creates desired or unwanted feelings. These participants exhibited physical/emotional sensations, or lack thereof, due to the beliefs they hold of their experience without a father. For example, faulty perceptions of the situation were, "Since I did not have a dad I will not be a good dad" and "My dad left me because I am not a good son." Healthy beliefs included, "Not having a dad will make become a better dad to my son," and "My dad left because had he had issues that did not involve me." These beliefs, impact the participants physical/emotional states, not the absence of their father.

**Perceptions of Paternal Absence**

The second category Perceptions of Paternal Absence is comprised of 4 themes. These themes include: *1) Significant Memories of Father, 2) Fluidity of Perception and Feelings, 3) Current Perception of Father's Absence,* and *4) Acquired Values Related to Absent Father.*

Participants were able to disclose their current perception of their father. These perceptions were classified as negative, neutral, or positive. Some participants discussed hating their father because of his absence; others were more understanding and had no aversive thoughts regarding the situation. Most interestingly were the participants who had no knowledge of their father or why he was absent. The ambiguity of their father relayed no aversive thoughts or feelings towards him.

In the attempts to describe the perception of their absent father, participants utilized specific memories to portray a personal understanding of him. The memories disclosed in this study were also connected to the feelings/perception each participant has of his absent father. Painful memories accompanied negative perceptions, while neutral/pleasant memories followed corresponding understandings of their fathers. Utilizing a memory to describe their father was a personally acceptable strategy to express their perception of paternal absence, and thus, its effects on their lives. Expression of a memory directly associated with a perception shows the potential of changing how someone views their father. If an individual can identify pleasant memories of their father, the possibility of a corresponding positive perception becomes greater. As seen in the data, these memories do not have to be one's own; they can be memories that family members disclosed or positive beliefs an individual creates to challenge negative or irrational perceptions.

The evidence in this research suggests the fluid nature of perceptions. Participants explored the notion that their understanding of their absent father changed over time. Beliefs which once impacted participants' mood and behavior have been challenged and subsequently dismissed or reevaluated. The fluidity of perceptions suggests an individual may not always have a negative opinion of his absent father; such a transformation may be achieved through personal growth, understanding, and the willingness to alter cognitions. The situation itself will not be altered, rather, what changes are the beliefs and perceptions held of the absent father. An evolution of ideas allows an individual subsequently adopt new beliefs of their father, themself, the situation, and the future.

The experience of growing up without a father has allowed participants to adopt certain values and beliefs regarding themselves and the life they want to live. Some participants have made the decision to become better fathers, while others have strived to for success in their education and careers. Although the values and beliefs differ, the variable of an absent father remains constant. Adopting values related to their experience is an important phenomenon that impacts their feelings towards their father and themselves.

**Feelings towards Father**

The third category Feelings towards Father is comprised of 5 themes. These themes include: *1) Current Desire for One's Father, 2) Dynamics of Current Feelings towards Father, 3) Feelings Regarding Father's Absence, 4) Childhood Feelings towards Father,* and *5) Connecting with Absent Father.*

The participants in this research described their feelings towards their father when they were a child. Many felt anger and resentment while others expressed curiosity and ambiguity. The connection between childhood feelings and behaviors is a concept worth noting; as children many of the participants did not know how to verbally express their feelings. Consequently, their behaviors were expressions of their feelings, often displaced.

Participants also expressed their current feelings towards their father. Many of the participants had neutral and/or positive feelings towards their absent father. Some participants had negative feelings while others felt a both positive and negative feeling; which is classified as combined. During the interviews many of the participants attempted to take an optimistic stance towards their father. They tried to express positive feelings but eventually expressed repressed anger and frustration. Attempting to take a positive stance towards their father is an example of the dynamics that occurs with the feelings of an individual who grew up in a single parent home.

Such dynamics were also seen in the participants' attempts to manage their feelings. On the surface, there appeared to be conflicting emotions related to the participants' absent parent. The "combined" category showed negative and positive feelings towards their father. The data helped to clarify the difference between one's feelings towards their father and feelings towards the reason the father was absent. Almost all of the participants expressed angry towards their father's absence; not towards the father. Words like: "pissed," "upset," and "hate," were used to explain their feelings towards their father's absence. This is an important classification that participants were able to understand which allowed personal insight into their own experience; the difference between the way they feel towards their father and the way they feel towards the situation.

There are also two identifiable dynamics expressed in the participants' feelings towards their father. "Processing," or working through their feelings, is a way participants were able to change the way they felt towards their father. Displacement of aversive feelings is the second way some participants managed their experience; the anger they felt towards their father was unacceptable, thus, the feeling was placed on a non-threatening object. For example, a participant expressed anger towards cigarettes. His father had been a long time smoker and did so throughout the participant's childhood. This is one participant who was understanding of his father's absence but expressed extreme anger towards the one aspect he hated the most. The individual did not allow smoking in his home and threatened to leave his fiancée if she continued to smoke. This is seen as displaced anger which was initially directed at the participant's father; however, it was transferred to a non-threatening, more acceptable object (i.e. cigarettes).

Many of the participants in this research showed no desire to have their father return to their lives. However, the desire to have one's father was accompanied by ambiguity surrounding his absence. The participants who did not know the reason their father was absent wanted to reconnect with him and develop a relationship. Those who had negative or positive feelings towards their father were content with his absence and wished to maintain the distance. However, participants desired to have some sort of communication with their father (phone/email) but did not want them back in their lives. They have lived without their father and have adapted to the situation; having the father return to their lives appeared to be a stressful thought which worked against their current state of self-preservation.

Some participant expressed fear, not knowing how they would feel if their father returned; others felt they had "moved on" and desired to live their lives, "without looking back." The desire to have contact with their father at a distance shows the impact such a relationship can have on their lives as well as the fragility of their emotions surrounding the his absence. This concept also highlighted and the individual's capacity to express personal needs as well as the desire to preserve current emotional functioning.

**Coping without a Father**

The final category *Coping without a Father* is comprised of 6 themes. These themes include: *1) Childhood Behaviors, 2) Perceived Effects Related to Father's Absence: Motivation, 3) Feelings of Self: Maladaptive Cycle and Avoiding Self Hatred, 4) Parenting: The Importance of Paternal Modeling, 5) What makes a Family, 6) Father's Day.*

As discussed in the prior category regarding childhood feelings towards father, participants further explored their behaviors in the absence of what is commonly known as "the disciplinarian of the family" (Montare & Bonne, 1980). Participants discussed the impact their father's absence had on their lives and their behavior. Participants explained much of their behavior to be a coping mechanism which allowed them to manage their feelings.

Some participants had the opportunity of retrospectively observing their behavior before and after the father left the home. They described being a normal child who felt secure and confident. However, when their father left the home, they became angry and aggressive towards their family, peers, and self. The insight into behavior pre and post paternal absence highlights the correlative nature of the two variables. Although these individuals may have had other stressors in their childhood, their father's absence impacted their behavior and emotional functioning. Other participants described "feeling angry all the time," "wanting to be away from home," "staying out on the streets," and "getting into fights." These are seen as ways participants coped with feelings and perceptions of their fathers.

Insight into the participant's experience is found in Atkinson & Ogston's (1974) description of the emotional impact of a father's absence, as well as Montare & Bonne's (1980) description of a father being the disciplinarian. Experienced strong emotions, such as anger and fear, accompanied with the lack of a disciplinarian figure, can illicit aggressive and acting out behaviors. The emotional toll of growing up without a father and the absence of the father's direction can create an environment for pathological behaviors. Combined, an internal state and external environment pull for certain behaviors. It is not the absence in itself, however, the perception of the absence and the emotional response to such a perception which creates detrimental childhood behaviors.

The participants also described the effects this experience has had on their lives and their ideology. They described utilizing their father's absence as motivation to become a better human being. Aspects of their existence such as work-ethic, parenting, and general morality were impacted by the absence of their father. This phenomenon is another example of Ellis's (1995) REBT; the event is not as relevant as the accompanied beliefs or perceptions. Participants chose to utilize their experience by adopting beliefs/values which have the capacity to create constructive or destructive behaviors. In this research, beliefs adopted by their experience facilitated behaviors such as "becoming a better parent", "finding a second job to support the family," "being there for my kids and wife," and "having a respect for fathers who raise their children."

Discussing participant's feelings of themselves was another theme that emerged within this study. Many participants explored their feelings of self to be related to their experience without a father. Two aspects emerged within this theme; avoiding self-hatred and the history of a maladaptive cycle.

There has been a longstanding effort for the individuals in this study to identify positive aspects of themselves in order to decrease self-hatred. Those who expressed anger and aversive feelings towards their father, at one time or another, directed the same feelings towards themselves. A conscious effort to avoid hating oneself has been another way participants understood the connections between their feelings of their father and their feelings of themselves.

Participants were also able to identify a maladaptive cycle of paternal absence in their genealogy. They expressed a consistent family lineage where mother's raised their children alone. Participants expressed a unanimous desire to change this cycle regardless of their feelings and perceptions of their absent father. This desire is also seen as a way participants changed and managed their views of themselves. Although they are a part of a family where many of the children were without a father, a realization and decision emerged, consequently raising their children and improving their self-image.

In their attempts to deconstruct a maladaptive cycle and cope without their fathers, participants adopted beliefs surrounding the importance of a paternal/male role model for all children. They also described the idea that their father's absence, will in part, make them better parents. They agreed that although their father was not present, his absence was a parenting tool in itself. They discussed the notion of learning what not to do as a parent by observing their father's lack of influence on their lives. This is a key factor in this research; participants' perception of their experience has impact on their current and future behavior. They commit to learning from mistakes made in their family and use them to improve their parenting as well as themselves.

In attempts to cope without their father's, participants found themselves becoming closer with other family members as well as family friends. They described what they believed family to be and how family should treat one another. Many participants explained family to be, "people who are there for you" and "those who you can trust." The ideas and beliefs these participants hold allow them to trust others and engage in healthy familial relationships. If they held the belief that their family members would abandon them, like their father, participants would not be able to have such enriched relationships out of fear and distrust. This highlights how beliefs and perceptions have influenced the participants' lives and behaviors.

Of the nine participants, all reported differences in their perceptions, feelings and attitudes towards themselves, the situation and their father. The main factor influencing these changes within all participants is *age*. As the participants matured, they were able to separate emotion from their experiences and evaluate their perspectives and positions regarding the absence of their fathers.

### Theory of Fatherlessness

This research's general conclusions affirm Ellis's (1995) theory of perceptions being more important than actual situations. Ellis's theory can be generalized to diverse experiences which show perceptions and beliefs to impact individuals' thoughts, feelings, and behaviors. The situation's impact can be controlled by altering cognitions related to each event. In the case of this research, participants showed beliefs surrounding their absent father that impacted the way they developed, understood themselves, chose relationships, and viewed the world. From the data five theories are presented:

1) An individual who was raised without a father, who also does not understand the absence, may create a self-damaging perception of the situation, and intern, present with ambiguity of self and surroundings.

2) An individual who has created a perception of their father's absence, of which, does not contain self-blame, will have a healthy view of themselves and their surroundings.

3) An individual who has a negative perception of their father and his absence will foster deep rooted anger towards the situation. Since the object of the anger is absent, such anger is sublimated in a healthy manner or released onto self, relationships, and/or other family members.

4) An individual's perception and feelings towards their absent father lie on a continuum from negative to positive. Perceptions and feelings can and will change throughout a lifespan.

5) A person's beliefs and perceptions of their absent father has more of an impact on their life than the absence itself.

## Clinical Implications

The present study has taken an approach that identifies cognitions and emotions in relation to the understanding of the father that plays a role in the individual's life. It is not enough to place responsibility on a father for leaving the home, clinicians need to understand how the absence of a father influences the thinking and emotional state of an individual.

There are many uncontrollable factors that cause a father to leave the home. Some of these reasons are consequences of war, death, divorce, imprisonment work and a host of others. Since the roles of psychologists are not to force a father to stay with his family, we must look at the individual's personal struggle without a father in order to decrease adverse symptoms. By identifying this struggle, a clinician may be able to alter faulty cognitions and perceptions of the self and others.

Another clinically relevant aspect of this research is the identification and utilization of defenses which individuals employ to cope with the absence of their father. One defense highlighted in this research is displacement. It will be essential for clinicians who treat individuals raised without a father to identify defenses utilized as a child, and as an adult, in order to understand and treat their patient. It will be important not to suddenly strip the patient of their defenses; they have learned this behavior as a survival tool. Instead, clinicians must teach new ways of coping with feelings and stressful situations, consequently decreasing the need for and strength of the engrained defense.

Dealing with emotions and perceptions are major components of therapeutic treatment. This research identified the impact perceptions and beliefs have on an individual's mood and psychological functioning. In treatment, patients must be made aware of the impact each perception of their father has on their emotional stability. It will also be important to identify the relationship between the perceptions of an absent father and ones views of themself, their environment, and their future. The fluidity of perceptions noted in this research allows patients to understand beliefs can be altered and perceptions can be changed. In doing so, the patients feelings towards their father and themselves can also be changed.

Noted in the results and discussion sections, participants current feelings towards their father differed from those as a child and adolescent. Patients in treatment must also be made aware of the fluidity of their feelings in regards to their father. Although patients may have aversive feelings towards their father, there remains the possibility that such emotions can be transformed with conscious effort and understanding.

The general clinical relevance of this research explains the impact a father's absence has on a child/adult. Dealing with any clinical issue, a therapist must consider if an absent parent has played a role in the development of maladaptive behaviors and/or pathological emotional/psychological functioning. Clinicians must convey the message that if an individual is distressed by anything external (or internal) the pain is not due to the thing itself but to their estimate of it; and this they have the power to change at any moment.

## Limitations of the Study

This study has gathered a significant amount of data regarding personal experiences growing up without a father. It expanded on prior research surrounding the phenomenon of paternal absence. However, there are limitations to this study that hinder its complete exploration of the impact perceptions of fathers have on innumerable variables.

This study only looked at the male's experience without their father. Consequently, the data and conclusions can only be generalized to males within the age group that was sampled. This study did not address populations such as; females, older adults, adolescents, and children. These individuals will have had a different experience than adult males and it will be important to explore their perceptions without a father in order to proceed with any conclusions.

An inability to generalize this research to all males is another limitation of the research. The predetermined number of participants was eight-ten; it is possible that saturation may not be met due to this limited amount. The sample also consisted of males who lived in Southern California; Los Angeles and San Diego. This region of the United States differs from others in the country and in the world in areas such as culture, ethnicity, socioeconomic status, weather, and variables that affect perception and experience. In order to get a more defined set of conclusions for males without fathers; a larger number of participants need to be sampled from different locations around the world.

Another limitation to this study surrounds the type of data gathered. The researcher inquired about past experiences, the data may have been skewed due to the complications of memory retrieval and the inability to describe experiences as they happen. The researcher relied on the participants' memory and their verbalization of their childhood. It is possible the experiences may have been somewhat altered through time.

Time is also another limitation on the study. In regards to family dynamics and underlying emotional issues surrounding a father's absence, a one hour and thirty minute interview is not enough time to gather a complete understanding of an individual's childhood an adult experience.

**The Researcher**

Since the researcher is a graduate student in a Psy.D. Clinical program, it is important to note the level of experience the researcher has had. Studying qualitative methods requires a person to take an in depth examination of an experience. The researcher is learning this process and may have some biases, prejudices, or lack of experience that may influence the data.

To minimize the effects of these limitations, the researcher took an empathetic position throughout the entire process; from initial research question, to data analysis, to the final discussion. While interviewing the participants, it was be important to show empathy and withhold judgment so the participants experience was explained without feeling judged. Having a researcher uncover deep rooted emotional and perceptual data regarding family requires a high amount of trust in the researcher. It was important to show the participants that the researcher is very interested in them and their experience, and ensured the quality of their disclosure to be acutely presented.

As a researcher, he may have his own bias towards this phenomenon that may have affected the way he look at the data and the questions he asked the participants. The researcher was raised in a home with his father and mother. However, he grew up in an environment where the majority of peers were raised by a single mother or grandparent. The researcher saw differences in his behavior than those of his peers who grew up without a father. This personal experience may have had an impact on the way the researcher addressed the study as well as the manner in which he looked at the data.

The finale limitation surrounds the researcher's gender. Since the researcher is a male, he might have evoked or suppressed emotions within participants as they described their experience. It will be important to note that a researcher of a different gender and age may have identified different responses and asked different questions. The researcher is aware of his impact on the research and attempted to minimize his influence on the data.

## Directions for Future Research

This research approached the phenomenon with a qualitative method of inquiry. Other methods may render various results, and thus create different conclusions. A researcher may take the approach of observing individuals who were raised without a father in different environments. As a method to enrich the data, a researcher could also observe children in the home and their interactions with their mother. Quantitative styles of research can measure factors such as perception, self-esteem, stress, depression, and issues surrounding the experiences of paternal absence. It will be important to address this issue of absent fathers through various perspective which will further the understanding of individuals' experience.

As mentioned in the limitations of this research, it will be important to explore different populations and their experience without a father. Women and men may differ in their perceptions and feelings surrounding their absent father, it will be important to identify these differences and explore this research from women's perspectives.

This research attempted to identify perceptions as a component in experiences without a father. However, there are many other factors that change an individual's environment as a result of an absent father. Research surrounding the change in environment and specifics that are impacted by the father's absence will be important to consider. Further understanding how an individual organizes themselves around this environment, as well as identifying behaviors that such environment pulls from the individual, will further the knowledge of those who grew up without their fathers.

Another aspect of relevant inquiry would be to examine the participants within this study at a later date. The researcher would like to interview the participants ten to twenty years post initial interview. This will be done to examine potential time specific differences in the participants' beliefs, perceptions, emotions, and any other factors related to their lives that may have a connection to experiences related to an absent father. It will also be beneficial to examine/interview the participants alongside their primary caregiver. It can be assumed such interviews will be highly emotional and provoke data different from that which was discovered in this research. Such data will illicit experiences from the caregiver that can be cross examined to the initial participants. This data will also provide a clearer understanding of how the initial participants' perceptions were influenced by their primary caregiver.

References

Amato (1994). P.R. Amato , Father–child relations, mother–child relations, and offspring psychological well-being in early adulthood. *Journal of Marriage and the Family,* 56, 1031–1042.

Angel, R., & Worobey, J. L. (1988) Single motherhood and children's health. *Journal of Health and Social Behavior, 29,* 38-52.

Atkinson, B., & Ogston, D. G. (1974). The effects of father absence on male children in the home and school. *Journal of School Psychology,* 12 (3), 213-219

Averett, S. L., Gennetian, L. A., & Peters, H. E. (1999). Patterns and determinants of paternal child care during a child's first three years of life. *Marriage & Family Review, 29,* 2-3.

Bateson, G. Jackson, DD, Haley, J., & Weakland, J.(1956). Toward a theory of schizophrenia. *Behavioral Science,* 1, 251-264. 23

Battle, J. (2002). Longitudinal analysis of academic achievement among a nationwide sample of hispanic students in one-versus dual-parent households. *Hispanic Journal of Behavioral Sciences*; 24: 430 - 447.

Beaty, L. A. (1995). Effects of paternal absence on male adolescent's peer relations. *Adolescence, 30,* 873-881.

Bengston, V.B. & Roberts, R. (2002). How families still matter. NY: Cambridge

Bianchi, S. M. (1995) The changing demographic and socioeconomic characteristics of a single parent families. In Hanson, S. M. H., Heims, M. L., Julian, D.J. & Sussman, M. B. (Eds.,) Single Parent Families: Diversity, myths and realities (71-97). New York: The Hawthorne Press.

Biller, H. B. (1993). *Fathers and families: Parental factors in child development*.
Westport, CT: Auburn House.

Biller, H. B. (1982). Fatherhood: Implications for child and adult development. In B. B.
Wolman (Ed.), *Handbook of developmental psychology* (702-725). New
York: Wiley

Biller, H. B., & Meredith, D. L. (1974). *Father power*. New York, NY: David McKay.

Biller, H.B. & Weiss, S.D. (1970). The father-daughter relationship and the personality
development of the female. *The Journal of Genetic Psychology,* 116, 79-93.

Blankenhorn, D. (1995). *Fatherless America: Confronting our most urgent social
problem.* New York, NY: HarperCollins.

Bogels, S., & Phares, V. (2008). Fathers' role in the etiology, prevention and treatment of
child anxiety: A review and new model. *Clinical Psychology Review*, 28(4), 539-558.

Botta, R. & Dumlao, R. (2002) Communication patterns between fathers and daughters
and eating disorders. *Health Communications*, 14, 199-219.

Braun, K. Helmeke, C. Ovtscharroff, W.J. (2006). Lack of paternal care affects synaptic
development in the anterior cingulate cortex. *Brain Research 1116 (1): 58-63.*

Brewaeys A., Ponjaert I., Van Hall E. V., & Golombok S., (1997). Donor insemination:
Child development and family functioning in lesbian mother families. *Human
Reproduction, 12*, 1349-1359.

Broude, G. J. (1990). Protest masculinity: A further look at the causes and the concept.
*Ethos, 18(1)*, 103-122.

Cabrera, N., Tamis-LeMonda, C. S., Bradley, B., Hofferth, S. & Lamb, M. (2000).
Fatherhood in the 21st Century. Child Development, Millenium Issue, 71, 1, 127-136.

Clarke-Stewart, K. A. (1978). And Daddy makes three: The father's impact on mother and young children. *Child development,* 49 (2), 466-478

Crockett, Eggebeen, & Hawkings (1993). L.J. Crockett, D.J. Eggebeen and A.J. Hawkings , Father's presence and young children's behavioral and cognitive adjustment. *Family Relations,* 14, 355–377.

Davis, E. C.,&Friel, L. V. (2001). Adolescent sexuality: Disentangling the effects of family structure and family context. *Journal of Marriage and the Family, 63,* 669-681.

Dornbusch et al. (1985). S. Dornbusch, J.M. Carlsmith, S.J. Bushwall, P.L. Ritter, H. Leiderman, A.H. Hastorf and R.T. Gross , Single parents, extended households, and the control of adolescents. *Child Development,* 56, 326–341.

Eberhardt C.A. & Schill, T. (1984). Differences in sexual attitudes and likeliness of sexual behaviors of Black lower-socioeconomic father-present vs. father-absent female adolescents, *Adolescence,* 19(73), 99-105.

Ellis, B.J., Bates, J.E., Dodge, K.A., Fergusso, L., Horwood, J., Pettit, G.S. & Woodward, L. (2003). Does father absence place daughters at special risk for early sexual activity and teenage pregnancy? *Child Development,* 74, 801-821.

Ellis, A. (1995). Changing rational-emotive therapy (RET) to rational emotive behavior Therapy (REBT). *Journal of Rational Emotive & Cognitive Behavior Therapy* Volume 13, Number 2, 85-89, DOI: 10.1007/BF02354453.

Elelman, M. W. (1987) *Families in peril: An agenda for social change.* Cambridge, MA; Harvard, University Press.

Fagan & Iglesias (1999). J. Fagan and A. Iglesias , Father involvement program effects on fathers, father figures, and their Head Start children: A quasi-experimental study. *Early Childhood Research Quarterly,* 14, 243–269.

Folstein, M., Folstein, S.E., McHugh, P.R. (1975). "Mini-Mental State" a Practical Method for Grading the Cognitive State of Patients for the Clinician. *Journal of Psychiatric Research,* 12(3); 189-198.

Fritsch, T. A., & Burkhead, J. D. (1981). Behavioral reactions of children to parental absence due to imprisonment. *Family Relations, 30*(1), 83-88.

Gerson, K. (1993) No man's land: *Mens' changing commitments to family and work.* New York: Basic Books.

Gould, Shaffer, Fisher & Garfinkel (1997). M.S. Gould, D. Shaffer, P. Fisher and R. Garfinkel , Separation/divorce and child and adolescent completed suicide. *Journal of the American Academy of Child and Adolescent Psychiatry,* 37, 155–162.

Griswold, R.L. (1993) Fatherhood in American History: A History: New York: Basic Books

Harper, C.C., & McLanahan, S.S. (2004). Father absence and youth incarceration. *Journal of Research on Adolescence*, 14, 369-397.

Hetherington, M.E. (2003). For better or worse. NY: Norton.

Hetherington, M.E. (1972). Effects of father absence on personality development in adolescent daughters. *Developmental Psychology*, 7(3), 313-326.

Horn, W. F. (2002). *Father facts*. Washington, DC: National Fatherhood Initiative.

Hosley, C. & Montemayor, R. (1997). Fathers and adolescents. *The role of the father in child development*, NY: Wiley, 162-178.

Hymowitz, P. (2007). Child custody disputes in adoption cases: Safeguarding the relationship with the psychological parent. In J. Aronson (Ed.), *Understanding adoption: clinical work with adults, children, and parents, Family Process*, (79-91), Lanham, MD:

Jaffee, S. R., Moffitt, T. E., Caspi, A., & Taylor, A. (2003). Life with (and without) father: The benefits of living with two biological parents depend on the father's antisocial behavior. *Child Development, 74,*109–126.

Johnson, D.J. (1996). Father presence matters: A review of the literature. *National Center for Families on Fathers.*

Kesner, JE, & McKenry, P.C. (2001). Single parenthood and social competence in children of color. *Families in Society*, 82, 136–143.

Knox, D., Zusman, M., DeCuzzi, A. (2004). Effects of divorce on relationships with parents. *College Student Journal,* 38, 597-601.

Krieder, R. M., & Fields, R. (2005). Living arrangements of children: 2001. *Current Population Reports,* (pp, 70-104, Table) Washington, DC.: US Census Bureau

Lamb, M., E. (ED.). (2004) The role of the father in child development (4th ed.). Hoboken NJ: Wiley.

Lamb (2000) The history of research on father involvement: An overview, *Marriage and Family Review,* 29, 23–42.

Lamb (1977a). The development of mother-infant and the father-infant attachments in the second year of life. *Developmental Psychology,* 13, 637-648.

Lamb (1997b) The development of paternal preferences in the first two years of life. *Sex Roles, 3, 495-497.*

Leonard, M. (1966). Fathers and daughters. *Internat. J. Psychoanal.,* 47, 325-333.

Paterson, J., Pryor, J. & Field, J. (1994). Adolescent attachment to parents and friends in relation to aspects of self-esteem. *Journal of Youth and Adolescence,* 24(3), 365-376.

Pleck, J. H., & Masciadrelli, B. P. (2004). Paternal involvement by U.S. residential fathers: Levels, sources, and consequences. In M. E. Lamb (Ed.), *The role of the father in child development* (4th ed., pp. 222-271). New York: Wiley.

Pleck, E. H., & Pleck, J. H. (1997). Fatherhood ideals in the United States: Historical dimensions. In M. E. Lamb (Ed.), *The role of the father in child development* (3$^{rd}$ ed., pp. 33-48, 314-318), New York: Wiley.

Maine, M. (2004). Father hunger: The impact of fathers on daughters. NY: Gurze Books.

Marino, C. D. & MCCowan, R. (1976). The effects of parent absence on children. *Child Study Journal,* 6 (3), 165-181

Marsiglio W, Day. Randal., Lamb., M. (1997). Exploring fatherhood diversity: Implications for conceptualizing father involvement. *National Council on Family Relations.*

Marsiglio, W. (1995c) Young nonresident biological fathers. *Marriage and Family Review,* 20, 325-348

Maykut, P.S., Morehouse, R. (1994). Begininning qualitative research: A philosophic and practical guide. Falmer Press; London and Washington, D.C.

McLanahan, S.S., & Teitler, T.O. (1999). The consequences of father absence. In: M.E. Lamb, Editor, *Parenting and child development in "nontraditional"families,* 8, 83–102.

McLanahan, S., Garfinkel, I., Reichman, N., Teitler, J., Carlson, M., & Audigier, C. N. (2003). *The fragile families and child wellbeing study baseline national report.* Princeton, NJ: Princeton University, Bendheim-Thoman Center for Research on Child Wellbeing.

Medinnus, G. (1965). Delinquents' perceptions of their parents. *Journal of Consulting Psychology, 29* (6), 592-593.

Mintz S. (1998) From Patriarchy to androgyny and other myths: Men in Families (3-30) Mahwah, NJ: Lawrence Erlbaum Associates

Montare, A., & Bonne, S. L. (1980). Aggression and paternal absence: Racial-ethnic differences among inner city boys. *The Journal of Genetic Psychology*, 137, 223-231.

Mulkey, Crain, & Hamington (1992). L.M. Mulkey, R.L. Crain and A.J.C. Harrington , One-parent households and achievement: Economic and behavioral explanations of a small effect. *Sociology & Education,* 65, 48–65.

Patton, P. Q., (2002). *Qualitative Research & Evaluation Methods 3$^{rd}$ Edition.* Thousand Oaks, London: Sage Publications

Popenoe, D. (2000). Ideology trumps social science. *American Psychologist, 55* (6), 678-679.

Quinlan, R.J. (2003). Father absence, parental care, and female reproductive development. *Evolution and Human Behavior.* 24(6), 376-390.

Richard, F. D., Bond, C. F., Jr., & Stokes-Zoota, J. J. (2003). One hundred years of social psychology quantitatively described. *Review of General Psychology*, 7, 331-336.

Rubin, L.B. (1976). Worlds of pain: Life in the working class family. New York: Basic
    Books.

Sanford et al. (1995). M. Sanford, P. Szatmari, M. Spinner, H. Munroe-Blum, E.
    Jamieson, C. Walsh and D. Jones , Predicting the one-year course of adolescent
    major depression. *Journal of the American Academy of Child and Adolescent
    Psychiatry,* 34, 1618–1628.

Santrock, J. W. (1977). Effects of father absence on sex-typed behaviors male children:
    Reason for the absence and age of onset of the absence. The journal of Genetic
    Psychology, 130, 3-10.

Shulman, S., & Krenke, I. (1996). Fathers and adolescents. *College Student Journal*, 35,
    280-316.

Silverstien, L. B., Auerbach C.F. (1999). Deconstructing the essential father. *American

Psychologist 54*, (6), 397-407

Steinberg, L. (1989). Susceptibility of adolescents to antisocial peer pressure. *Child
    Development, 58*, 269-275.

Updegraff, K., McHale, S., Crouter, A., & Kupanoff, K. (2001) Parents' involvement in
    adolescent peer relationships. *Journal of Marriage and the Family*, 63, 655-668.

Walker, A. J., & McGraw, L. A. (2000). Who is responsible for responsible
    fathering? *Journal of Marriage and the Family*, 62. 574.

Wallerstein, J.S., & Kelly, J.B. (1976). The effects of parental divorce: Experiences of
    the child in later latency. *American Journal of Orthopsychiatry*, 46(2), 256-269.

Way, N. & Stauber, H. (1996). Are 'absent fathers' really absent? Urban adolescent
   girls speak out about their fathers. In B.J. Leadbeater&N. Way (Eds.), *Urban girls*:
   *Resisting stereotypes, creating identities* (pp.132-148). New York: New York University
   Press.

Wilson, S.C. (1982) Contact-promoting behavior, social development, and relationship
   with parents in sibling juvenile degus (Octodon degus). *Developmental
   Psychology. 15, 257-268.*

APPENDICES

APPENDIX A: INTERVIEW GUIDE

APPENDIX B: INFORMED CONSENT AGREEMENT

APPENDIX C: SUBJECT'S BILL OF RIGHTS

APPENDIX D: DEMOGRAPHIC QUESTIONNAIRE

APPENDIX E: FLYER

APPENDIX F: POTENTIAL REFERRALS FOR PARTICIPANTS

APPENDIX G: DATA; PARTICIPANTS THEME RELATED DISCLOSURE

APPENDIX A: INTERVIEW GUIDE

Study Title: The Perceptions of Fatherlessness:

Understanding the Development of Children's Perceptions of their Father's Absence.

Hello, I will be asking you a series of questions related to your experience growing up. These questions may bring up memories that you may have not had for a while. These memories may be pleasant, and/or possibly create some uncomfortable feelings. You have the right to decline to answer any question and/or take a break during this process. The validity of this study is heavily weighted on your responses, so please respond to them as open and honest as possible. Your participation is very much appreciated and I look forward to listening to your responses. Are you ready to begin? Once again let me know if you need to stop at any time.

1) **Self**

- So, can you tell me a little about yourself? (e.g., interests, life goals, hobbies, drug/alcohol use etc.)

2) **Family**

- Tell me about your family What are they like?
- Who do you consider your family?

3) **Relationships**

- What is your relationship like with your mother/guardian?
- What was your relationship like with your mother as a child?
- With any significant others
- Was or is there ever discussion about your father's absence?

- Describe your parents' relationship.

## 4) Experiences growing up

- What was your experience growing up without your father in the home?

- What were your feelings?

- How did you behave?

- Were there any significant adults in your life that played a role in your adolescence?

- What was your experience in school?

- How was your relationship with your mother/guardian

- How did you feel towards your friend's fathers

- When your father left, who did you spend most of your time with?

## 5) Feelings towards father

- What feelings do you currently have towards your father?

- How did you feel about his absence as a child?

- What emotions arise when you think about your father?

- Explain how would you feel if your father potentially came back into your life?

- What has motivated your feelings towards your father?

- Did your father use drugs or alcohol?

- Do you use drugs or alcohol? What role do those play in your life?

## 6) Perception/understanding of father

- Why was your father absent in your life?

- What was your experience not having a father?

- How do you feel about this reason?

- Has anything/anyone impacted the way you feel about your father?

- Has your perception changed from what it was as an adolescent?

- Are there any questions or concerns regarding your father's absence?

- Describe how your perception of your father's absence plays a role in your life?

- How did you understand his absence as a child?

- How did you currently understand his absence?

- What did you feel towards your father when you were a child?

- What words would you use to describe your father?

- Describe any memories you have of your father.

## 7) Effect of absent father

- Has your father's absence played a role in your life?

- What types of values do you hold?

- Describe your idea of a father? (Probe: Positive/Negative Father)

- If you could talk to your father today would you? (Why/Why not)

- What would you say?

## 8) Parenting

- Do you want to be a parent?

- What type of parent do you think you are/will be?

- What type of parent do you want to be?

- What is your perception of a man?

- What does fatherlessness mean to you?

## 9) Current feelings

- What is it like for you to be discussing your father's absence?

- How do you currently feel

- Explain any physical sensations you are currently feeling

- Is there anything else you would like to tell me regarding your experience without a father?

APPENDIX B: INFORMED CONSENT AGREEMENT

Study Title: The Perceptions of Fatherlessness:

Understanding the Development of Children's Perceptions of their Father's Absence.

You are being asked to participate in a study. This study is part of a dissertation in clinical psychology, which will be presented to the faculty of the California School of Professional Psychology at Alliant International University, San Diego. Before you consent to participate, please read the following and ask as many questions as necessary in order that you understand the conditions of your participation.

*Investigator*

Jody Adewale, M.A., Psy.D. candidate at the California School of Professional Psychology at Alliant International University. Dissertation chair of the Research Study: Gary Lawson, Ph.D. Professor, Lic.# 9547, California School of Professional Psychology at Alliant International University.

*Purpose of the Study*

The purpose of this study is to investigate a child's perception of his or her absent father and how it has developed. How does a child's positive, negative, or neutral perception of an absent father develop, does it have anything to do with the reason for the father's absence? In this study it will also be important to look at cognitive and emotional factors that have been components of an individual's perception of their absent father?

*Duration of the Participation in Study and Number of Subjects to Participate*

Your participation in this study will involve a short telephone interview and a one to two hour in person contact with the investigator to fill out a demographic survey and complete an in-depth interview. A minimum of eight participants will be involved in this study.

*Procedures to be followed during This Study*

Eligible participants will be contacted within forty-eight hours from the initial phone contact. At this time the interviewer will review the nature of the study, confidentiality, and informed consent. Upon verbal consent an interview will be scheduled. Participants will be informed that their information will be protected.

Upon arriving for the interview, participants will complete a Demographic Questionnaire. They will then participate in an in-depth interview that may take one to two hours to complete. The interview is semi-structured.

*Right to Decline to Participate or Withdraw from the Study at any Time*

Participation in this study is voluntary. If for any reason you decide to withdraw from participating in this study you may do so without any consequences. There will be a compensation of $20 for your time, regardless of completion of the Demographic Questionnaire or interview.

*Potential Risks*

The potential risk to you as a participant is considered to be minimal to moderate. It is possible that you may experience some distress or anxiety when discussing difficult experiences of your life. If you appear to become distressed during the interview, the investigator will stop the interview and remind you of your right to withdraw from the study at any time you wish.

*Potential Benefits of the Study*

Your participation in the study will help the investigator learn more about the experiences of those who have grown up in a home where their father was absent. The information that will be obtained for this study may contribute to a better understanding of how an individual's perception of their father's absence manifests itself in their current life.

*Confidentiality*

You have the right to privacy; therefore, all identifying information will be kept confidential unless disclosure is required by law. Your name and all identifying information will be changed to protect your anonymity and confidentiality. Upon completion of the study, all interview notes, audiotapes, and written transcripts of the tapes will be destroyed. The data collected from the interviews will be used in a clinical dissertation that will be presented to the faculty at California School of Professional Psychology at Alliant International University. A limit of confidentiality exists if you make statements indicating that you may harm yourself or someone else, or if you report current or past unreported child, elder, or dependent abuse. If such information is disclosed, a report will be made to the appropriate agencies.

*Permission to Audio Tape*

I must also be made clear that the interview session will be audio taped. Consent to participate in the research study includes consenting to be audio taped. The audio tapes and associated notes will be held in confidence and will be used only for the purposes related to the development of the clinical dissertation.

Documents will not contain participants name and some identifying information may be changed in order to protect the participants' anonymity. Only the researcher and the Dissertation Committee will have access to the audio tapes and that upon completion of the dissertation, the audio tapes will be destroyed.

*Questions about the Study*

If you have any questions that have not been answered at this point, the researcher will accommodate you to answer any questions or concerns. If you have any additional questions during or after the study, please contact the investigator Jody Adewale, M.A. at (323) 633-3892 or Dr. Gary Lawson, Lic.# 9547 at (858) 635-4748.

*Signature and Acknowledgment*

My signature below indicates that I have read and understand the above information, and I have had an opportunity to ask questions in order to understand what my participation involves. I agree to participate in this study and acknowledge that I have received a copy of this informed consent agreement and a copy of the Subject's Bill of Rights. I understand and agree that by signing this consent form for participation, I am not giving up any of my legal rights.

Signature of Participant: _____ Date: _____

Signature of Witness: _____ Date: _____

APPENDIX C: SUBJECT'S BILL OF RIGHTS

Study Title: Perceptions of Fatherlessness:

Understanding the Development of Children's Perceptions of their Father's Absence

As a participant in a research study you have certain rights and responsibilities. It is important that you fully understand the nature and purpose of the research and that your consent be offered willingly and with complete understanding. To aid in your understanding, you have the following specific rights:

To be informed of the nature and purpose of the research in which you are participating.

To be given an explanation of all procedures to be followed and of any drug or device to be utilized.

To be given a description of any risks or discomforts that can be reasonably expected to occur.

To be given an explanation of any benefits that may be expected to come to you as a result of this research.

To be informed of any appropriate alternative procedures, drugs, or devices that may be advantageous and of their relative risks and discomforts.

To be informed of any medical treatment, which will be made available to the subject if complications should arise from this research.

To be given the opportunity and encouraged to ask questions concerning the study or the procedures involved in this research.

To be made aware that consent to participate in this research may be withdrawn and participation may be discontinued at any time without affecting continuity or quality of your medical care.

To be given a copy of the signed and dated written consent form if requested.

To not be subjected to any element of force, fraud, deceit, duress, coercion, or any influence in reaching your decision to consent or to not consent to participate in the research.

If you have any further questions or concerns about your rights as a research participant, please contact your doctor.

## Appendix D: DEMOGRAPHIC QUESTIONNAIRE

Study Title: Perceptions of Fatherlessness:

Understanding the Development of Children's Perceptions of their Father's Absence.

Please respond to the following questions:

Full Name: _____

1. Sex: Male_____ Female_____

2. Date of Birth: _____ Age: _____

3. Ethnicity: Hispanic _____ Caucasian _____ Asian-American _____

   Native American _____ African American _____

   Other (specify) _____

4. Highest Education Completed: Grade_____ HS Diploma/Equivalent _____

   College _____ Graduate School _____

5. Employment Status: Employed _____ Unemployed _____

   If employed, what is your current job? _____

6. Yearly Income     Under $15, 000 _____

   15,000 – 29,999 _____

   30,000-59,999 _____

60,000-75,000 _____

Over 75,000 _____

7. Drug of choice: _____

8. Last Used: _____

9. Marital Status: _____

10. Children: _____

11. How old were you when your father left your family? Age: _____

12. Are you currently taking any medication for depression? YES    NO

    If yes please elaborate:

13. Do you currently feel depressed? YES    NO

    If yes please elaborate:

14. Are you feeling homicidal?    YES    NO

    If yes please elaborate:

15. Are you currently feeling suicidal? YES    NO

If yes please explain:

16. Are you taking any medications for any psychotic symptoms? YES   NO

    If yes please explain:

17. Do you currently see or hear things that other people do not?  YES   NO

    If yes please explain:

APPENDIX E: FLYER

Study Title: Perceptions of Fatherlessness:

Understanding the Development of Children's Perceptions of their Father's Absence.

Volunteers needed for a doctoral dissertation studying persons who were raised with an absent father.

If you are a male between 21 and 35 years of age and, were raised in a home where your father was absent, you are eligible to participate in this study.

This doctoral dissertation project includes an interview that will take approximately one to an hour and thirty minutes with an advanced doctoral candidate in clinical psychology. A licensed psychologist is supervising this study. Your participation may provide information that will aid in better treatment and understanding of those who were raised in a fatherless home.

If you are eligible and agree to participate, you will receive <u>$20 in cash</u> as compensation for your time.

To find out if you are eligible for this study, please call: Jody Adewale, M.A. (323) 633-3892.

APPENDIX F: POTENTIAL REFERRALS FOR PARTICIPANTS

JOSE CHERBOWSKY, Ph.D., MFT (MFC 41717)

Offices in Carmel Valley and San Marcos

(760) 420-4971

CAROLYN GERARD, M.A., MFT

(858) 756-8171

12625 High Bluff Drive, San Diego 92130

1516 Front Street, San Diego 92101

www.Relationships4Life.com

CARRIE JAFFE, Ph.D. (PSY 18811)

12625 High Bluff Dr., #104

San Diego, CA  92130

(858) 208-9689

www.cjaffephd.com

AZMAIRA H. MAKER, Ph.D.

Clinical Psychologist (PSY 21570)

12625 High Bluff Drive, Suite 104

San Diego, CA 92130

(858) 531-1122

www.drmaker.net

JILL SILVERMAN, LCSW

Psychotherapist (LCS 23073)

Office in Carmel Valley

(858) 793-2400

www.counselingandtherapy.com

JONATHAN KRAMER, Ph.D.

Phone: (858) 780-0988

Toll free: (888) JKRAMER

PsychologistSanDiego.com

KARIN KRISTENSEN, Psy.D.

Clinical Psychologist (PSY 19524)

Mission Valley Office

3633 Camino del Rio South, Ste 204

San Diego, CA 92108

(619) 281-9552

APPENDIX G: DATA; PARTICIPANTS THEME RELATED DISCLOSURE

Category One: The Experience of Growing up without a Father

The following six themes within this category emerged from the interviews.

Theme One: Relationships with Mother

Jonathan:    "My mother and I, we have a good relationship. No problems, never argue never

have disagreements. It was good when I was a child to. I was always a good kid,

besides being a brat and missing school."

Willy:    "In every one's eyes…your vision becomes skewed for what you want to

see…but in my eyes there really wasn't a relationship with my mom. After she

left my dad she was a youngster so she would try to catch up on her mid-twenties.

They would drag her home some nights piss drunk and that's all I remember. All

the clubs that she likes…to me, working at the club is my way of fighting off my

daemons from her… because I was there controlling what she used to be…I made

it harder for people like her to come out. I do have a relationship with my mom

but the damage of the past is done."

Robert:    "My relationship with my mom is weird. Like um, we love each other but we

don't show it a lot. You know?"

Steve:    "When I was a child from 8 years old till now it was always an open relationship.

We could talk about whatever we wanted; girls, school, career. Now that I am

married she more worried about my relationship. She has taken that father role.

She tells me how to treat my wife and how to act in certain situations. This is more like what a father should do. What guys would get from their dad. You usually can't get this kind of parenting from a mom. My mom played both roles for us. We really didn't need to have a father."

Ruben: "My relationship with my mom is now better than it has ever been. Sometimes I feel like she is my girlfriend where we fight and bicker at times but I appreciate her and I love her. It is stronger now than it was in high school. Before that when my dad left I was really supportive. Paul (participants brother) didn't really know how to handle it. He was more off to the side. My middle brother did not know how to deal with the situation. When my dad left I became more open and affectionate with my mom. What's weird is I taught her how to be affectionate. Like I was very affectionate with her, I would sleep with her at night in the same bed. I see it as my brother had lots of hatred to my dad so he just shut it out. I think he would hold anger towards my mom because he had to take care of the family. He had to get a job, so when he would look at my mom he would think "fuck, I have to work because you couldn't make your marriage work.""

Ravon: "My relationship with my mom is great."

Mike: "My mother and I are very close. We have a great relationship. We check in with each other at least once a day… My relationship was good with my mom as a kid. She was gone a lot and I was usually either with her or alone at home."

Paul: "My relationship with my mom is pretty good. But we had a big falling out. She still treats me like a kid I had a girl come over the house, we were raised never to do that but my friend couldn't drive because she had been drinking, So I brought her home and my mom made scene. I had to remind my mom that this is my house. Nothing really happened but it hurt our relationship. Our relationship was still the same but it was tough seeing her struggle and not open up to her sons. I feel she needed a daughter to talk to. My mom doesn't communicate, but as a child it was pretty good."

Eloy:    "My relationship with my mom is good but it is kind of like an older sister to me. We are always ragging on each other. I feel like were friends more than a mom and a son. My mom and I had a rough relationship when I was a teenager. Her friend passed away and she stopped taking care of herself and let the house go."

Theme Two: Discussions about Absent Father

Jonathan:    "To tell you the truth not even ten times. Well I had my own father, there are five of us and my other siblings have different fathers....there was never a real discussion about our fathers. Coming up I never really asked about them."

Willy:    "Yea I talked to my grandparents about my father leaving. I talked to my mom all the time about my dad too...but there were always negative things about him. The only thing she would say positive was that my dad would provide for me and the fridge would always be stocked with food....I would say thanks for feeding me but where is the emotional stuff that I need...where is my hearts food?"

Robert:    "No, never. I already knew. Shit, he was in and out of prison. I just knew at a young age you know. They never really talked to me about it. My mom never did. I knew already."

Steve:     "My mom told me that he had a family on the side. When my mom told him that she was pregnant he said, "Here is Ten thousand dollars, go take care of it." Ten grand later, I'm still here and his money is no where to be found. She made the right decision…I have accomplished a lot. I have nothing to prove to him. I am married, I have a decent job. But I hated that he thought he could get rid of me for 10 thousand dollars, that's all I was worth to him? As a child I never really asked about my father because I was so used to living without one. I started asking about him when I knew he was alive."

Ruben:     "I wouldn't necessarily say there was ever a discussion about my father's absence. When my mom would talk to me about my dad I would block it out."

Ravon:     "No, there was never a real discussion about my dad. I mean they talked about him but it was like where is he at? They wouldn't really talk much about him, just how he used to be back in the day. No real details. It wasn't till I became older until I started to learn about who he really was."

Paul:     "Not immediately when he left but eventually there was a discussion about my father. I was encouraging my mother to meet people and date so she wouldn't be alone. But she has not and she will not. So we didn't really talk about him, more just how she should forget about him."

Mike:     "I think there was a discussion about my father when I was a kid. He used to make a lot of promises that he did not fulfill…My earliest memories are of my mother taking me to go see him in prison. So we basically talked about it. She would say, "Your dad is a good guy, we just did not get along." She was real direct with her feelings and the reality of the situation. She would tell me, "Just because he is like that that does not mean you have to be lie that, you are going to grow up and be something." She wanted me to learn from their mistakes."

Eloy:   "Yea, when I was little I always talk about wanting a dad. I would see my friends playing catch with their father and I wanted that. My mom would talk about my father and what he was like; but I just wanted him around."

Theme Three: Childhood Experience without a Father: Parentification and Defenses

Jonathan:   "Bad! Just like overall…two boys in the house growing up without a father. I never cried over him. I never went through those situations where I cried for him, I kind of just pushed it out."

Willy:   "I don't know. I blocked most of the stuff out from my childhood. There was something that happened really bad when I was a kid…it's the type of thing that you don't want to ever happen to a kid….It was like completely crossing boundaries…there was a point where I wanted to find him (participant's father) and obliterate him. I wanted to find a way to blow him up into pieces because he was not there to protect me from this other man. I can remember being so angry and I can remember what the pain felt like. I was so pissed that he wasn't there. I would clinch my fist and people could see the anger I had towards my dad."

Willy:   "I didn't have shit. I had to figure out the way the world works because I had to raise myself. Since I realized who I was I was able to understand the world."

Robert:  "It was messed up for a little kid, at a young age. I started doing a lot of wrong (Participant laughs); for my dad and with my dad. As a little kid I never shit...what do I say...I was grown up quick bro, I learned things quick. Yea, I had to take care of myself. I didn't like it but...I had to deal with it...I was pissed off. He would miss my games and shit like that."

Steve:  "As a child I was on my own. My mom worked three jobs and I was always alone. It was an interesting way of being; I mean being on your own all the time with no adults. I grew up real quick. In high school I worked more. I wish I could go back and had the opportunity to pursue my dreams instead of having to grow up so fast because I had no adults in my life. I would have had that pressure of having to find a job because I have to help pay rent. I could have gone back to school and done anything. Growing up I would hear my friends talk about their dad and how their dads would do things with them and teach them how to ride a bike or skateboard. I didn't have all that. So for me it was like ok, that's cool, whatever. I would bug my mom for these things but I knew she couldn't and I didn't have time for those things because I had to work...When you grow up in a home without a father you don't have a male figure to attach to. So you are going to look for something else to attach to, it could be good or bad, but you will find something to attach to."

Ruben:  "My experience without a father was empowering. I was the spoiled child, but when my dad left I had to take all these responsibilities. My parents put me in a rough spot, they made me decide who I wanted to live with. That was one of the hardest decisions of my life. I have to be in control, I can't live with the unknown, my father had a lot of that in his life."

Ravon:  "No body, like none of my cousins grew up with, had their father so it was like a normal thing. If you didn't see your father then it really didn't matter because no one in the community had their dad. I guess you can say that my experience was normal, normal as can be. It's not like I could tell what was missing by not having a dad. No one had a dad…All the male influences in my life were negative influences. That may have helped to pull me away from all the negative influences, because all the male influences were all negative. I learned what not to be. They were always in front of us, but the type of mom I had would shield us away from that and try to keep us doing right."

Mike:  "Not having my father had its goods and its bads. I feel a father can either make or break your future and a bad dad who is around can really hurt you. So I see it is somewhat of a blessing that he was not around to affect my life. My dad was also abusive. He would be on drugs and we somewhat had to escape from his abuse. I would have loved to have him around to teach me to play football and ride a bike but the reality is that it is best that he wasn't around. When I saw other people's fathers I felt fucked up. I was like, "Dam, where my dad at?"…I have a memory where I was still in a walker and he left me and ended up getting arrested that night. I was left alone at home and I walked out of the house in the walker by myself. As a kid I saw the edge of the side walk and stood out there by myself for 10 minutes. Eventually my mom came by and saw me on the street. I feel pissed off when I think about this. Who leaves their kid in a walker, by themselves, in a house? At that moment I realized I had to take care of myself."

Paul: "My dad passed away in 2001 and she still hasn't moved on. I wish she would date; she needs someone to spend the rest of her life with. I feel like she is under my care, and I don't want all the responsibility…It was tough. It made it really hard on me. I almost dropped out of school. Emotional it did not affect me because he and I never saw eye to eye. I have always been independent so I did not rely on him. I started working and buying my own cloths at the age of 12, I learned I could take care of myself. What was tough was the financial burden he left on my mother and my younger brothers at the time…and me having to pick up that slack, that father slack. I had to be the father of the house. I had to pay bills and keep a full time job."

Eloy: "When I was a child we lived in a trailers park and my mom called me over to help her out with a problem. There were possums in the restroom that she could not catch and I needed to help her. We could only catch on of those possums and we decided not to use the restroom anymore. From then on, I had to plan my shits and showers around my schedule. Like I would brush my teeth at Carl's Jr. every morning and shower in the locker room at school. If my dad was around he would have been able to take care of things like this for us. I grew up so poor, we would have to sleep in a dilapidated room with a broken mattress. I felt like I had to hide this from my peers."

Theme Four: Talking about Absent Father

Jonathan:     "It feels good to talk about my dad. I never really talked about it. I never got this
              deep. I never do this with anyone. I was uncomfortable talking to other people
              about this kind of stuff. I used to feel uncomfortable talking about my father. But
              now I am able to talk about him."

Willy:        "It feels good to talk about my father and not rage. I am able to know it is in my
              past. The pain is so dull now. I am now noticing how far I came in thinking about
              my father."

Robert:       "This shit is pissing me off talking about this shit. I don't like talking about the
              shit he has done, but I like talking about him and remembering him."

Steve:        "I am comfortable talking about my dad. It feels good to talk about my dad. I
              have to let it off my shoulders. Years ago I was angry about it and did not want to
              bring it up, but now I realize that I have to talk about it, or I am going to live with
              all this anger."

Ruben:        It is fun to talk about my father. I feel good, I have accepted the situation. I have
              accepted him and appreciate him as well as the situation. I was given the
              opportunity to stop the cycle. To improve the males who have the same last name
              as me."

Ravon:        "I have no problem talking about my dad."

Mike:         "It feels good to talk about him, like I am doing now. I am in a comfortable space
              where I can really talk about it" (pertaining to his father).

Paul:       "I feel indifferent talking about my father; it does not bring up anything for me."

Eloy:       "It feels good to talk about my father. I did see a therapist for a little bit and I

found it helpful, much like this, we just talked about my experience without a

father."

Theme Five: Experiences in School

Jonathan:    "From K-6 I had no problems. I loved school. From 7-9 I was running around, not

taking school serious. The only thing that kept me going to school and not

dropping out was basketball. When I was younger I could have just stayed home.

I never went to school but when I got serious with basketball I really started to

want to go to school. During $6^{th}$ grade I had to "will" myself to go to school. In $5^{th}$

grade I would show up like at 11 or 12 every day. My school was only 1 block

away and I never went to school. My teachers would be like "why are you even

her. I would only show up for a half day for almost the whole year. I could sleep

in till I got up when I wanted to get up. Around $6^{th}$ or $7^{th\ grade}$ BCW (child

protective services in New York) would come around trying to take me and my

brother away from my mother because we were missing school so much. So my

mother started waking us up to go to school. The reason I wasn't going to school

was because nobody cared. My mother didn't really care."

Willy:       "I was always awkward. I was off my melon. The way I would dress...I didn't

want these people around me and the easiest way was to wear black. I didn't want

anybody to get close to me. I used my weight to intimidate people. This kid once

hit me over the head with a book...I waited outside of his house with a

switchblade ready to cut out his heart…I hid behind his house but he didn't come
out and I cried. I wrote him a letter and told him I was going to rip his hear out
and eat it just so I can understand why he was being such a bitch to me. Every
time I had a problem with someone I would imagine them just like my dad. I
would twist things…like when this guy hit me over the head with a book…I
would say…maybe my dad would hit me over the head with a book…if he never
left me he would probably hit me over the head too. I would have grabbed him
and slammed his head into the wall. They kicked me out of school because I
fucked up this guy in high-school. Then at the second high-school I chucked some
guy off the second floor and jumped down to finish him…there goes that fit of
rage again. I didn't want people around so that why I dressed the way I did. I
gained weight because I knew that no one was going to feel up the fat kid. I was
the weirdest and craziest kid in school. This is what made me feel valuable. It
made me feel important. If you didn't know me personally, you at least knew
who I was. People would know that I was crazy but they would look beyond that.
I can still be a social misfit but still have people around. It worked."

Steve:      "School was fun, yet it was entertaining for me. Watching people grow. They
would always talk about their family. They would always talk about their dads
and their family. I was very observant of people when they would talk about their
family and their dad."

Mike:       "I had to deal with his absence because it fucked with me as a child and as an
adult. When I got to college I had to deal with feelings of being inept. I used to
feel like I wasn't good enough to be at college. I used to see my behavior,

bickering with my coaches and other students as a reflection of inadequacy stemming from my father being gone. If my dad was around he would have helped me through these times when I didn't know who I was. I would do great on my tests and I would understand all the information in school, but there was this constant nag in my head that told me I didn't belong there and I was inadequate. But around my junior year I started to figure it out and tell myself that I can make it."

Theme Six: Significant Adults who were Supportive

Jonathan: "My mother and my uncles played a role in my life; also my aunt and my grandmother. My uncles played a father role in my life. They would discipline me and put that fear in my heart. My uncle would keep me in check, he was the disciplinarian. My uncle would always be right there."

Willy: "My aunt and my uncle played a role in my life. They seemed perfect to me...I felt comfortable and safe...they didn't judge...that's where I got my personality from...the good parts...my aunt would always encourage me and say "no matter how weird they are they will accept you for you."

Robert: "My uncle, He was my mom's brother. He was like my dad too growing up. When I was a kid, like nine years old, that's when I learned how to drive bro. I taught myself how to drive. Even if my dad was in or out, I would drive over there (his uncle's house). Any chance I got I would go to my uncle's house."

Steve: "Around age 12 I had my best friends dad who was kind of a father figure, he would give words of advice.... I also felt very curious about my father. But my mom would fill that void. She would take me to sign up for baseball and karate. She made sure I had what the other kids had, except for a father figure."

Ruben:     "My girlfriend's father has become a positive role model for me. I have become close with him over time."

Ravon      "My Uncles, aunts played a large role in my childhood. I talked to them every day."

Mike:      "There was this one boyfriend of my mom who was around from age 6 to age 9. He was the one male ventral role model in my life. He was the longest most prolific male in my life and he only lasted 3 years."

Paul:      "Nissum (participant's childhood football coach), he was like my father and played a role in my life where my father left that void."

Category Two: Perceptions of Paternal Absence

Theme Seven: Significant Memories of Father

Jonathan:     "My father left when I was ten. I only saw my father 1 time in my life. I remember the day. He came in the morning and my mom was like your father is here. He would always promise to come but he never did. Then one day my mother was like "your father is here, and I ran and hugged him. It was exciting for the first time to see him. He stood around for like 2-3 days and I probably spoke to him 3 times after that. It felt like Christmas seeing him. I was super surprised when he came. When he didn't come I wasn't depressed or surprised, I just expected him to disappoint me. It wasn't anything to depressing. I really stopped caring and I started to say I will believe it when I see it. However, That first day I say him we didn't do anything special. I was just by his side all day. We just walked through the neighborhood all day. I don't really have any other memories of him."

Willy:     "I have no memories of my father. He was gone 26 out of the 28 years of my life."

Robert:    "The bad memory was…. always going with him and stealing and shit. At the same time I was a little kid and knew what he was doing. I hated it, but back then I knew I was going to get broken off with some money. He would bribe me. Just that shit, that's a bad memory, you know, seeing him overdosing and shit, him getting arrested and shit. No kid should see shit like that, lot of bad but a lot of good too. Another memory was when I was little, we were at some party and there was some dude, younger than my dad just started talking shit. He was on him all day. Since I was there my dad really didn't do anything. So my dad told me to take a walk and go down the street. He was calling him punk bitch, fucking punk bitch. I heard all this going on and I was a little kid. I knew what was going to happen already and I was scared as fuck. My dad whooped the shit out of him. I told my dad, "What happened? Why did you do that? What's a punk?" He told me, "Don't let anyone ever call you a punk." So I took that to the heart, because my dad told me, you know. It could have been good or bad, but since my dad told me, I took it to heart. Shit, growing up, I just hated when people would call me a punk."

Steve:    "When I was 11 years old I found out I had a father. Growing all the way up to 11
          years old I thought my father was gone, dead. They told me he was dead. But
          when I was 11 someone pointed him out to me. Some said, "Hey look, that's your
          dad." When they showed me my father I did not believe it. I cried and ran out of
          the restaurant. It was a shock."


Mike:     "When I was playing football at USC, I used to see guys on the team and their
          father's would stay with them after practice and help work on their technique. I
          remember watching those situations and think, "Damn, it would have been nice to
          let my father be there to see his son on the team." I felt sad for him, because he
          could have enjoyed this with me."

Paul:     "One memory of him pissed me off. My dad never came to see me play
          basketball but he only came when he found out I was good. He starting coming
          only when he found out I was good on the court. One game against Fremont, I
          had the best game of my career: 23 points, 6 blocks. Fremont was a good school
          too. But back then the LA Times cover much of the high school basketball and I
          came out on the cover after this game. I was really excited and had the paper at
          home. When I woke up in the morning the paper was gone and I asked my mom
          where is it; I really wanted that paper. My mom told me my dad to it to work to
          show off to his friends and brag about me, even though he never came to see me
          play. That pissed me off. He wanted to show me off but he was never there to
          support me."

Ruben:     "There are only a dozen memories I have of my dad. There is a lot of stuff that I have blocked out of my head, I mean, memories of my father. He used to play with me but only for a minute; like he didn't really want to be around me. I also remember him forcing me to go to his baseball games on the weekends which I found miserable. This is probably why I dislike baseball so much. There was always a struggle between me and my father. He wanted me to play baseball and I wanted to play football and basketball. I guess I hate baseball because of my father…After he passed away, when we were burying him, it was weird. Other people would tell us how all these kids loved him and how he was so good with other kids. This pissed me off so much. It pissed me off because I am his son but he was spending time other kids. But in my work, I am able to see how my father would come about doing this. I sometimes see kids where I work and I feel bad for them. I fell they need some extra attention. So I could see how my father spent time with other kids rather than his own, because I have done it."

Ravon:     "I can only remember one memory about my father. It was at my brother's wedding and we talked about the wedding, not about why he left and that was it."

Theme Eight: Changes in Perceptions and Feelings

Jonathan:     "Overtime I got smarter, more mature, and more understanding of what is going on and why he left. My other brothers and sisters never had their fathers, so no one was going to feel sorry for me. They didn't have their fathers either. I let go of a lot of this stuff. That just me. My perception has changed a little bit form when I was a kid; putting all the information together. As a kid, he tried one time. I kept

talking till him a little bit and was curious about him.. He was trying when I was a
kid, and me being that age I am going to accept him at least trying. Now its just
different. If he called me today, I would be like, "I live over her call me if you
want to come and I will meet you at the airport." I wouldn't be all excited. As a
child I wasn't chasing him but I was looking, expecting, desiring, wanting to see
him. He was calling me. I wanted him to come around but I didn't try to go
where he was at. I wanted him to come where I was at. I still want him to come,
if I found information to get in touch with him."

Willy:       "My son has impacted the way I feel about my dad. Having my son helped me
realize how the father son relationship would be. He has made me realize how
much I want my father. My relationship with my son…him wanting to be with
me and wanting to play with me…makes me want to be with my father more. I
have never felt being wanted the way my son wants me. My son wants me so
bad. I used to look for that feeling in girls. I used to search for that so hard. That
love. Now I kind of hate them now and realize I don't need them anymore. I got
what I need in my son."

Robert:      "My son has helped change my feelings towards my father. Before my son I was
always pissed off, more anger. But after my son, I guess he  taught me to love my
dad more."

Steve:       "I got over the anger towards this guy. I met him one more time 2 years ago and
all the rage was gone. There was no point to it. He is not angry over me so why
should I be angry over him… Ever since I met my wife and got back into church I

don't hate my father as much. I don't have the anger or resentment towards him anymore."

Jonathan:    "Overtime I got smarter, more mature, and more understanding of what is going on and why he left. My other brothers and sisters never had their fathers, so no one was going to feel sorry for me. They didn't have their fathers either. I let go of a lot of this stuff; that just me. My perception has changed a little bit form when I was a kid; putting all the information together. As a kid, he tried one time. I kept talking till him a little bit and was curious about him.. He was trying when I was a kid, and me being that age I am going to accept him at least trying. Now it's just different. If he called me today, I would be like, "I live over her call me if you want to come and I will meet you at the airport." I wouldn't be all excited. As a child I wasn't chasing him but I was looking, expecting, desiring, wanting to see him. He was calling me. I wanted him to come around but I didn't try to go where he was at. I wanted him to come where I was at. I still want him to come, if I found information to get in touch with him."

Robert:    "My son has helped change my feelings towards my father. Before my son I was always pissed off, more anger. But after my son, I guess he taught me to love my dad more."

Eloy:    "My father is from Indian decent and his parents did not like my mom because she is not Indian. A couple of years ago I was looking around the house and found some letters from my dad to my mom. These letters said how much he loved me and missed me. I did not know my father had these feelings towards me. When I read them, it was honestly for the first time that if felt I had a father figure who actually loved me. This was hard evidence where this guy wrote how much he loved me and missed me. Obviously actions speak louder than words, and I understand the cultural issues that put distance between us. But when I read those letters, for the first time in my life I felt I had a father. It felt good not to carry that resentment anymore. Before I read those letters I knew I had a father but I never felt like I had a dad. I had no strong male influence at home, but I had uncles and teachers who I could talk to. The letters made me feel like I was not a burden that takes his child support every month. Before those letters I had some resentment towards Indian culture or anything Indian. It was a lot related to my father being Indian."

Eloy:  "The biggest thing that has impacted the way I feel about my father is the letters that I stumbled upon. I was astonished that my dad touched this piece of paper. He is not just some mythical guy out there but he is a human being. That was a turning point where my feelings sort of changed. This was just a year ago."

Theme Nine: Current Perception of Father's Absence

Jonathan:  "I don't know why my dad was not there. Maybe just moving on? I really don't know. He was married somewhere else and that's all I really know. I didn't even know what state he lived in. I was too young and my mother didn't really say. When I was young if you don't ask questions you didn't get answers. I was never really open with my mother where I could ask her things about my father. I could open up to my Aunt. She lived in the neighborhood and I could ask her questions about my father. We wouldn't dig deep or nothing. I wouldn't investigate about my father."

Willy: "He couldn't take it. It wasn't just him, my mom left him too. He thought, "if I stay here I'm stuck." I guess he didn't want to be stuck with me."

Robert: "My dad was gone because he was a drug addict. My dad was always a drug addict but he always had a job you know? But at the same time, being a drug addict and having a family and rent, and everything he had to do."

Steve: "My dad had a wife and another family on the side. Many men have mistresses, turns out my mom happened to be the mistress."

Ruben: "As I get to know more and more about my father, I start to understand that he had to be the way he was because he was raised in tough conditions. His life wasn't easy so I understand his way if being. My father did not know any better. This is not what people have told me but it is my reasoning, my own rationalization. For example, when it rains, some people would explain it as God is crying. Is God crying? No! But the reasoning makes people feel better and allows them to live with a situation they do not understand. It's the reasoning that has helped me."

Ravon: "Why was my father absent in my life? That I have no idea. Besides the fact that my mom said he was kind of selfish, and my mom told me that he already had a kid. But the real reason, I don't know. He never gave us the real reason why he left."

Mike:      "Ultimately, I feel my father was absent in my life because of his socioeconomic

status. He was a victim of his environment. He made multiple decisions that

ruined his life. The final case was the one that put him away. (Participant

reluctantly continues), the final charge was violence related with a fire arm. I feel

like this is fucked up but ultimately, I came out ok and had a great mom. I was

not the only one who went through it. Millions of guys go through not having a

dad. I feel blessed that at least my mom was there but I feel sad that society

creates these situations without it being necessary. I feel a character flaw

developed because of my father's environment…I would explain my dad as lost

and confused. He was barely a kid, he couldn't raise a kid. He was a young kid

who needed a father himself. He made a mistake; he shouldn't have had me that

young."

Paul:      "I consider my father being absent even when he was in my life. But I believe he

was absent because he was not a supportive father. He never truly (long pause)

was committed to his wife, my mother, he was never committed to us as children.

I don't think he loved he. He was never committed; he never wanted to buy a

house that is why we rented. If you buy a house that is commitment and he never

wanted to do that with us. When he left us he got with another woman who had

two kids, he took care of those kids when he had his own. He did not take care of

us but he took care of someone who wasn't his blood."

Eloy:      "My father chose not to be in my life. That's why he was absent. If you really

care about something you will be there, bottom line; that is not an excuse. His

cultural issues are valid but it is not an excuse for leaving his son. If he really wanted to be a part of my life he would be. It is difficult for me to answer that because I can't read his mind. But I am somewhat able to understand his mind."

Theme Ten: Acquired Values Related to Absent Father

Jonathan: "I am a good person, I am not the best father but I will try. I value family and friends. I value being a good father. I know how it is. I have two other sons in different states. He comes out here to visit me sometimes. And my cousin… I mean my son, I still talk to his mother all the time. I'm just like my father how he did to me and my mother. But times are different now. His absence did influence me but in a small role but not that much. Him not being there has not made me want to work extra hard to be around my kids because I am not working extra hard to see them. He hasn't really affected me to be a better father to my kids. I am here with my daughter right now and her mother and I am going to make the most out of this time."

Willy: "I value my time with my son…but it is hard to show…I have never had a man show me affection so I don't know how. I get scared because my son is very affectionate. It is extremely hard for me to be physically affectionate with my son. I get in defense mode when my son kisses me on my arm or gives me a hug. I snap out of it because I don't want him to end up like me. So I explain to him how uncomfortable it makes me feel and it is not that I don't love you. .. A lot of times when I do things I tell myself don't be like my father. My father being gone somewhat motivates my behavior."

Robert: "The only thing in my life that I value is my son. I have learned that a good dad is one who is around his son all the time, raising him, being with his son. I want to show him the ropes of life. The good ones you know… good values. Shit, it's not cool! (Participant laughs). Not having a dad…umm what can I say, every son needs a dad, the way I see it. Like I would not go to my mom for certain things, shit I needed to talk about and get off my chest. Every boy needs a dad."

Mike: "Fatherlessness…(long pause) means discarded. That's the first word that comes to my mind. When you are fatherless, it is like someone didn't care for you, didn't think enough of you and you are discarded. Its one thing if your dad died or was gone for a legitimate cause, but it says something when he can be there and you are still fatherless. I felt thrown away like a McDonald's cup. However, if you grow up without a father; you can still grow up alright. A lot of people have excuses and blame it on their father being gone, but if you have one solid parent you are doing a lot better than many other people."

Paul: "Your dad leaving really changes your life. It puts your life on a whole different path. I had to pick up his slack and I think it makes it hard on everyone when the father leaves."

Eloy: "I realized the resentment I have for my father could be used as a crutch and as something that I can use to hold me back. Or I could use the resentment and build myself up and make a better life for me and my family. I see lots of kids who use the hate for their father to do something destructive, but I realized I had to use it to better myself."

Category Three: Feelings towards Father

Theme Eleven: Dynamics of Current Feelings towards Father

Jonathan: a) <u>Neutral</u> "I don't have any feelings towards my father. Time heals all things. I am 33 years old and time heals all. It has been 23 years of time past since I last spoke to him so I have no current feelings towards him. Time has healed any anger towards him. I would be excited to see him but if I don't I don't really care. It's been twenty-three years, one more day is not going to hurt."

Willy: <u>Negative</u> "I told him if he ever sees me on the street cross the street because I will beat you up. I told him that I want him to be different so instead of wanting to beat him up, I go hug him and love him. But sometimes I think, "No dad, I made it this far. I'll do the same without you. I'm a fucking phoenix, you don't know me... In time my struggles will kill me but I'll rise from the ashes or fade from memory doing my best. I'm going to prove you wrong, wait for the confirmation to hit your ears from others because I am mute to you as well as deaf. I'm going to a do shit... I'm going to fucking do shit with my life!"

Robert: <u>Combined</u> "I have a little bit of sadness. Mad. Little bit of anger, but love too. Yea, (long pause) I knew my dad was a drug addict long before. That's when I started going with my dad places. I remember that day like it was yesterday. It was just me and him, I missed school and we were going to breakfast we went to go see his parole officer and right after that...a couple hours later...he was broke and shit...he had just got out of jail and hadn't got a job and shit. The way to survive was just to steal so...I remember it was me and my cousin and we were walking to home depot....this shit is pissing me off talking about this shit. My dad gave me like two drills. He gave my cousin two drills and he had two saws and we just walked out the fucking store. But I knew what was going on. But my cousin was like seven or eight. We just walked out. Nothing happened, we got in the car and left and I was thinking, "What kid has to do this, why me." My dad went to go sell that shit and we went to his friend's house, his friends were drug addicts. I'm not talking about drug addicts like you see on skid row...but...I don't know how to put it. Drug addicts are drug addicts. But they had jobs and were clean cut, like my dad. I thought that was the bottom you could go, having a kid steal shit. Ever since then I would miss school so he would not fall asleep behind the wheel and crash and shit. In other words, be the getaway driver."

Steve:      Negative "I did not even know that my father lived in the same neighborhood as me. That means when I was on the bus on the way to school, I could have been next to him. I could have bumped shoulders with this man and never even know. I found it fucked up. What an asshole. Now I find it hilarious though. I could have bumped into him so many times....As a child you hear a dad is supposed to do certain things for you, growing up to be a man, growing up to learn about life. You know, teaching you morals, teaching you boundaries. The resentment of looking like him comes from all that."

Ruben:      Negative "A lot of emotions come up when I talk about my father, anger disappointment, frustration. I am not going to say my father was the worst, but I can't say he was the best...Hearing this makes me sound like I am an emotional mess. I will cry for anything. I try to make myself tougher but I have allowed myself to become emotional. My son has directly affected the way I feel towards my father."

Ravon:     <u>Neutral</u> "I don't have any resentment or anything. I never knew any fathers so it was just normal not having a dad. There was never any anger or any resentment. I would just wonder and be curious mostly. I'm going off of TV. I would see people on shows having moms and dads and I would, I guess, I would wonder how that would feel. I was curious how it would feel to have a dad."

Mike:      <u>Positive:</u> "Honestly, being a grown man, I really have no ill will towards my dad. My mom explained it to me which made me feel better. My dad grew up in a home where his mom would drink and smoke weed with him. His mom would give him the drug supply to go sell at school to his friends. I am big on taking everything into account, and that is just what he knew. My mom told me that before he started taking drugs, he was a good father. He took care of me and she showed me pictures as a baby where I was asleep on his chest. He was cool. He just had a problem when he started crack and cocaine. I really am able to understand he was not able to cope. This helped me to understand that it is not good to avoid your problems. I have learned to address problems and take them head on. I saw my father as trying to run away from an issue. Everybody has their crutch, but I learned to address my problems…However, when I think about my father, feelings of disappointment and regret come up; disappointment because he failed me when I was a child, him being addicted to drugs. I realized he had a character issue. He would sober up in jail and when he would get out he would immediately return to using and not come to see his kid. That to me is a character issue. He would be out of jail, start using drugs again, then in 2 weeks be right back in jail."

Paul:    Neutral: "My dad is dead, but if he wasn't dead, I would not make an effort to talk to him because my life went in a totally different direction because of his actions; abandoning his family. I understand you don't want to be married to your wife anymore, but you have a responsibility to take care of your kids. It is hard to say I have feelings towards my father because he is dead. So it's like I should just let it go. But I still hold a little resentment for his actions. With time you learn to forgive, this resentment is not a potent and not a strong of a feeling as it was when I was a child…I think about him on a daily basis. But I don't sit and think about him, when I do think about no emotions come up."

Ruben:   b) Displacement "My father smoked cigarettes heavily and drank heavily. I hate cigarettes so much because of this reason. He would have yellow fingernails, dry skin, and that smell. When I smell cigarettes I think of my father. I would be very angry if my son started to smoke. I have smoked cigar, but the first time I did it in Miami I just did not feel comfortable. One thing I will not put up with in my life is family members smoking cigarettes; it's just my decision. Smoking is a trigger for me. When I smell cigarettes, I get triggered and all the resentment and bad memories come up."

Eloy:    Displacement "I have never really thought about my feelings towards my father. I really just used to blame my mother and be frustrated towards her. As I became a teenager, I started to feel that anger and resentment facilitated by not having a dad. I would direct some of that anger to my mom and I would think, "It is your fault (mom) that we are in this situation."

Eloy:      Processing "Right now I understand the pressures he was dealing with and his cultural issues. I understand his mother did not want him marrying a Mexican woman or any non-Indian woman for that matter. I read a story where a man in India decapitated his daughter because she was with a guy he didn't want her to be with. In India it is just a different way of living and I understand my father's absence. As I have gotten older, I have become to understand him more. It would be difficult for him to have us and still have his Indian family. It was much easier for him to just pay the 18 years of child support than balance out conflicting families. I have a lot more empathy for it than I did as a kind. But the bottom line is that he has a responsibility to me as his son to be there."

Mike:      Processing "My father had a son (participant referring to himself) who was an over achiever, I feel sad that he did not get to experience me. If I was a dad I would have loved to see a kid like me grow up and become who I am today. If he could have done it all over, he would have changed it. I don't feel anger towards him, I just feel sad that he made those decisions to ruin his life. I have thought about this and him for a long time. I had to figure it out.

### Theme Twelve: Current Desire for One's Father

Jonathan:   "If he came back into my life, I would feel another chapter would be opened. I don't know if I would call it closure but I would look at him and ask, where you been? I would want him to come back in my life."

Willy: "I want an attempt at reconciliation with my father. I learned that shit is trivial…everything get better with time."

Steve: "I would not let him in my life. I would not give him my number, email, address, I wouldn't give him anything. I wouldn't give him that pleasure…I don't want to go where I thought I was going as a child. It wasn't so much of a depression it was more being rebellious. I was wild. However, doing what I was doing help me, it helped me grow. When I have kids, there will be no way in hell that I will let them be like I was as a child. So that makes me a better person. I don't want that fool to put his two cents in mine."

Ruben: "When my dad left as a child it was empowering, when he died and I was an adult it was frustrating. I wanted to connect with him and start a new relationship but I was unable to. It was frustrating because I wanted to take control of a situation, but I couldn't."

Ravon: "I don't necessarily want him back in my life, I just want to know why he left? f I could talk to my dad I would want to ask him what's the point? Because I knew he had kids with other women and I would like to ask him what is the point of abandoning his kids and why would he abandon all three of us?"

Mike: "If I could talk to my father today I probably would not. I really don't feel like dealing with the emotional baggage that he probably is going to have. I'm cool, but I can see him being overly emotional and I don't want to deal with all that. He told my uncles that he wanted me to go see him. But why the fuck would I go see him now, I am 25. Like if was really trying to be apart of my life he would

have sent for me when I was in fifth grade. But if I had to talk to him I would not
ask my dad about why he left or talk to him about my experience growing up
without him. You see, we need to let the past go. We are in the future and if I had
to talk to him I probably would not dwell on the past. I would discuss his feelings,
how is he coping with adjusting to a new world where their son when was a child
when he last saw him; now he is a man."

Eloy:      "I would like to think that I would be welcoming towards my father if I saw him.
I would not completely ignore him but I wouldn't let him easily back into my life.
I am somewhat neutral on my feelings towards him. It is like where was he when
I needed him. I don't need him now. I would want to meet my half siblings more
than my father. I actually feel more empathy for them and I don't understand
why...maybe it's a way of feeling sorry for myself."

Paul:      "I am adult now, so, him coming back into my life wouldn't affect me. I am set in
my path. However, I wouldn't let him be a part of my life. I wouldn't confide in
him and I wouldn't search him out."

Theme Thirteen: Feelings Regarding Father's Absence

Jonathan:  "I wanted to know why he wasn't there. Maybe he didn't live in New York, I
don't know. I do want to know the reason why he wasn't around. It doesn't really
bother me though."

Willy:     "I think it was cowardly that my father wasn't there for me when I was a child.
He was not ready to take care of a life but here was there to conceive one. That's
what makes him a coward. You can't sit there and not feel anger towards my

father. When I think about him and I am alone, I write my emotions down, I write how I feel. I write down my anger. That was just bull shit…if you are going to lay down with a woman…you better be ready to take care of your kid. Right now I have a neutral feeling towards my father's absence…before it was negative…it has never become positive. But because of the fact that it changed, I would not be the person I am today. It changed and I changed."

Robert:     "Um I'm pissed. Seeing all the shit I did when I was a kid. And not having him around. No one had to tell me your dad was a drug addict you know. Shit I would miss school a lot to drive my dad around because he would nod out or fall asleep behind the wheel, so he wouldn't crash. My feelings towards my father's absence are, positive and negative. You know like, I know he is gone and I got accept that but um pissed. I'm happy he isn't in pain but I mad because he is not here because of the shit he has done. Like he did it to himself bro, so I'm pissed off too."

Steve:      "I just think it made me better. I grew from it. I was able to move on. What could I do cry like a little kid. The tears have been gone they have been shed but I had to grow from it. As a man I had to grow., and as I grew so did my hatred towards my father. Watching all my other friends have fathers feed my hatred towards my father. But now I have positive feelings regarding my father's absence. It gives me something to prove to myself that I don't want to be anything like him."

Mike:       "My father being in jail really fucked with my mind (Participant then presented with delayed speech, and proceeded to put his head down. Participant had difficulty discussing his father in jail). I felt like it made me want to always watch my actions because I could end up there…It was not like my dad was a fool. My dad was a very successful drug dealer. At least these Columbians and mobsters put some money away for their families. My dad didn't do that. He went and blew all of his money and left nothing for his wife and kid. My feelings towards my father were neutral because I understand his life as a child and he had a tough situation growing up. But as a man you have to take responsibility for your actions. So now it is negative, I have a negative opinion towards him."

Paul:     "Regarding my father's absence…I think it is weak. He was a conformist. He was content with the basic things in life. I am the opposite. I have a negative perception to his lack of commitment. However, he was disciplined and a hard worker, much like me. How do I feel about his death? I wouldn't wish death upon anyone and I am not happy that he is dead. But that is life, I am not broken up about it. I am pretty neutral about his death. Indifferent you could say."

Eloy:     "I am somewhat neutral on my feelings towards him. I think it is unfortunate that my father wasn't able to make up his own mind about choosing who he can have a family with. I do feel hurt about this reason but I have come to accept it and deal with it. It pissed me off at first but I have come to be more empathetic towards him. Towards his culture, I am frustrated. I have this feeling of being powerless, and I can't change the Indian culture but I want my dad. I have conflicting feelings, my whole life I have grown up not liking my father but as I have gotten older, I have learned to adopt the philosophy that shit happens for a reason. I would not want anything to change. I don't know who I would be or where I would be if he was around so I am appreciative of the person I have become."

## Theme Fourteen: Childhood Feelings towards Father

Jonathan: "Sometimes I wanted to see him I wanted to know who he was. I wanted to see what kind of person he was. I had a desire to meet him...I don't know how I felt when I was little. I just went on with my life. My other never really talked about him. My aunts always asked about him and I gave them the same answer, I don't know where my father is. I guess I was frustrated. I never had anyone who understood me or got me. Most of my friends had their fathers and they could go see them. I felt no one understood me."

Willy: "It was rage! I had rage towards my father!"

Robert: "I would try to act like I didn't care you know. It would bother me. I was just pissed off bro! You know. At the same time I knew he had to do what he had to do, but...I was still pissed."

Steve: "There was a lot of resentment for him. It was all because I didn't have my dad. I would often get depressed, I had a dad who was alive but I didn't have one physically next to me."

Ravon: "Curiosity played a role in my life when I was younger. I didn't know how to feel so I was just curious about him, who he was, where he was, and just him as a human."

Mike:      "As a kid I had more of a "fuck you" personality towards my father. The fact that

he wasn't there wasn't the problem with me. The fact was that when he was in jail

he would write me and promise that we were going to spend time together. But

when he would get out he would leave me sitting there, not call and not show up.

So when he would call after all this, I would be like "fuck him." It was not my job

to try, he is the father. If her is not going to try then I am not going to give him the

opportunity. I had a closer relationship with him when he was in jail than when he

was out, probably because he had to sober up. When I think about my father,

feelings of disappointment and regret come up; disappointment because he failed

me when I was a child, him being addicted to drugs. I realized he had a character

issue. He would sober up in jail and when he would get out he would

immediately return to using and not come to see his kid. That to me is a character

issue. He would be out of jail, start using drugs again, then in 2 weeks be right

back in jail…My father being in jail really fucked with my mind (Participant then

had very slowed speech, and proceeded to put head down. Participant had

difficulty discussing his father in jail). I felt like it made me want to always watch

my actions because I could end up there."

Eloy:      "As a child I had conflicting feelings towards my mother, at times she was my

world and other times I found myself frustrated and annoyed with her. As a kid I

was confused, I did not understand why I was the only kid without a father. I

wanted to go to ball games and play catch. I couldn't do these things and I didn't

understand why. As I became a teenager, I started to feel that anger and resentment facilitated by not having a dad. I would direct some of that anger to my mom and I would think, "It is your fault (mom) that we are in this situation."

## Theme Fifteen: Connecting with Absent Father

Jonathan:     "Yes, I would like to just find out information about him. How old is he, is he married, where does he live? It wouldn't be any anger or frustration. I am past the angry point you could basically say. The angry point was at the beginning when I was a child. When he would keep disappointing me and never show up. I wasn't in my teens more like when I was ten years old."

Willy:        "If my dad were to come back into my life I would eat that day up, like if it was a buffet. I have been waiting for that for so many years. Just for him to realize his mistakes and say I am sorry. I want him to try to make it right. I could be 60 and him to come in my life and from that day on try to make it better, I just want my dad."

Steve:        "Currently I just want to talk to him. I actually told my wife, because of my religion I want to talk to him and give him the benefit of the doubt. I have to go in there with an open mind and an open heart, because if he says something about my mom I can't hit him. The possibility of losing my job is too great and I would not lose it because of him. In the past the possibility of swinging on my father if I saw him was huge; but not anymore…If I were to contact him I would want to know why my father offered my mom money to get rid of me when she was pregnant with me. This is what I am angry about. This is what started all my anger towards him."

Ruben:     "If my dad came back into my life I would definitely want to sit down with him and talk. But I wouldn't ask him questions about why he left and our past. I would catch him up with my life and tell him about his grandson. I would not want him to be my father but more be the grandfather to my son. I think since I have accepted his absence and understood it; I am better equipped to cope with it."

Mike:      "I thought about going to see my father in jail, but at this point I would be indifferent to him. I know he is my dad, but I have got this far without him. He has not had any effect or imprinting anything on my life; whatsoever, on anything I have done. I would let me dad have my phone number, but I don't see how he would be a part of my life. I would not take the effort to allow him back into my life. That would take away the focus on what I am trying to accomplish."

Paul:      "If I could talk to him I would. I wouldn't confront him or anything."

Eloy:      "No I am not really interested in contacting my father. I would not really be interested in what he is doing. If I were to run into him, I wouldn't want to ruin his family."

Category Four: Coping without a Father

Theme Sixteen: Childhood Behaviors

Jonathan:  "Growing up in New York City you automatically hang out with a lot of people. I did what most of the people did around me. I had millions of friends; drug dealer friends, athletic sports friends, a bunch of different friends. I never sold drugs."

Willy:	"As I grew up without a father I had to look happy all the time because people start questioning you when you are sad. I would wake up some days and say to myself "today is going to be a shitty day." I'm tired of hearing about your perfect life and your cookie cutter life…your whole Andy Griffith show bull shit…I know you have a perfect life and my life is fucked up."

Willy:	"Back then there was a trigger point where I would flash back to crazy stuff and I would get violent but as that was going on I was going through therapy and I learned that I had to be ok with my father leaving me. I have to know that I am good without him…so when I get triggers to thinking about him I don't flash back and hurt someone I care about."

Eloy:	"As a kid I had times where I would act out and get aggressive. But usually it was just towards my mom…if my dad would have been around I think I would have acted different, but sine he wasn't there I was like I can do whatever I want, because he is not going to do anything."

Robert:	"I never was a bad kid, but I tried to be always on the street, never wanted to be inside. Yea, when he was gone I would act a fool you know, out of anger but I could also do what I wanted to do. But like when he was out, he straightened me out. But now, I am a fucking grown man, but I still need my dad to tell me shit, that's what I don't got right now."

Steve:	"Before I knew my dad was alive I behaved like a regular child; do my homework, play around, clean the house. I had rules. After I found out my dad was alive I started to wild out a little but… I became rebellious. I thought, if he is around where is he. When I was fifteen I wanted to talk to him. I was like I am a man and he is a man, why can't I talk to him. When I was eighteen same thing, same at twenty-on; I am close to thirty and I have yet to ask this man why he left me."

Ruben: "Before my father left I was a normal kid when my dad was around. I knew I had the potential to be whatever I wanted to in life. I used to be very laid back. School came easy to me. But when my dad left I took the responsible role when my dad left. At 11 years old I did really well in school and I started getting really focused. My brother dealt with it one way and I dealt with it in another way. At this time my mom used to cry herself to sleep. I would go and lay with her and hold her and tell her it was going to be fine. I would wait till she fell asleep then I would feel comfortable enough to fall asleep. I was comforting my mom."

Ravon: "I was pretty good kid. I never really got in trouble and it wasn't really that serious."

Mike: "I had a gradual progression. I used to get into so many fights; I used to have a huge temper. Any person who would say anything to me that was offensive, I would punch them."

## Theme Seventeen: Perceived Effects Related to Father's Absence: Motivation

Robert: "I have learned to just be a cut throat kind of guy because my dad was gone. I learned that I needed to take care myself however I can and to forget everyone else. I was angry at him and I found that I took my anger out on him onto other people but I am learning how to deal with my feelings and know that even though my dad was in jail it is possible that he is still a good man and loved me…when he died I found myself not as angry at him like I was when he was in jail"

Steve:  "I can't be emotional with another man when he talks about kids or fathers because I never had that. Also, if my dad was around I would have been more motivated. But overtime his absence became a motivation for me to better myself…Him being gone makes me want to be an amazing father. I am going to be there and make sure that I did everything he didn't do for me. Now that I am married I have to make sure I am not him at all. I reference all my negativity towards him. I don't want to be anything like him, I don't want any part of him in my life."

Ruben:  "Hell yea, my father's absence played a huge role in my life. How could it not? Even though my dad is not here, his absence is parenting me. Even relationship wise, I have gone above and beyond to make sure I don't give my son a broken home."

Ravon:  "Yes, my father's absence played a role in my life. For instance, I would never abandon my kids. He used to call us when we were younger and say he was coming over but never come through. For this, I would ever lie to a kid. I will always be a man of my word and maintain integrity."

Mike:  "I have an appreciation for men who take a responsibility for their kids. I have empathy for males who don't have a father in their lives and are trying to strive and achieve the right way. This is apart why I mentor other children. His absence has made me evaluate my decisions and my life a little more."

Paul: "I am the man who I am today because of all the experiences I have gone through. I faced all those things and overcome all of those obstacles much like a domino effect. Because of his initial action, I have become the man I am."

Eloy: "I see my father as any other dude. That has one thing that has motivated me to be so career driven, family oriented and all about success, because I don't want to be just any other dude. I don't want to be like him."

Willy: "When my son says, "I love you daddy," that would trigger the fuck out of me! I would not be able to hear someone say I love you like that. I even had my girlfriend just say she cares about me but don't say I love you. In regards to relationships with other people, I have never heard anyone say.. "you are a fucking ass hole I don't want to talk to you." Its always been the opposite. You look like a build scary wilder beast, then we get to talk to you and hear your views and you are a delightful person. All you think about is other people and you never put yourself first. People know I am can be a violent person, but they tend to know that I am a much deeper person and I am able to feel for other people and make sure they know that they are understood."

Theme Eighteen: Feelings of Self: Maladaptive Cycle and Avoiding Self Hatred

Willy: "As bad as I am there are good things about me. But it is hard coming out of twenty-six years of my life...well really my whole life of not having a father figure and then trying to be one. I want be a productive member of society and I cant. It weighs on you. It is a big weight on your soul and your mind that you cannot perform as a man should. I value the male role and I want to perform as a male should. I just wish I had my father around to show me how a man is supposed to act and live."

Steve: "It is easy for me to be emotional, but I sometimes feel it is not a good characteristic to have. It allows me to relate to people and if you cannot relate to people then you cannot be a good person. Sensitivity can be a downfall as well. I had the hard shell up for so long and just recently I was able to let my sensitivity and emotions come out."

Ravon: "I would describe my father as selfish, because of this; I wouldn't describe myself as selfish. I am selfish to a degree but not to the point of abandoning my responsibilities."

Ruben: Maladaptive Cycle "I think I am a father that is struggling to live up to his own expectations; I want to be a father who is working to improve himself and his family…I was absent for a year and a half from my son's life. I was a coward back then. I did not want to be a father and was in denial. I had to make a conscious effort to be in denial. I would drive to her house and wait outside week after week and never go knock on the door. I would want to just leave the bull shit and be the father I know I can be. I had another relationship and we were talking about having kids. But I already had a kid and I saw myself becoming my father. I was continuing the cycle, I told myself this is something that I would never do but her I was doing it. So I had to make an effort to change. When I made the decision to step up and be a father it was because of my dad. I was mad at myself because in some ways I became him. If I would have gone with what was easy I would have become my father. But I realized I was not him, so I came back home to my son and his mother. I was scared to be like my father, I was scared that I was going to fail as a father. I was scared that I was not going to stop the cycle and I was not going to be good enough; that's partly why I was not around. I still carry that fear but I constantly have to challenge it."

Ravon: Maladaptive Cycle "One thing I did learn about him and about him leaving us is that his father did the same thing to him. It was like a cycle. I sometimes worry that I'm going to do the same thing but I'm not really trying to have kids right now."

Mike: Maladaptive Cycle "My dad fell into the footsteps of his dad. My grandfather was a lot like the way my dad was. I don't want to be like that and I don't want to continue that cycle."

Paul: Avoiding Self Hatred "My father was a hardworking and complaisant and selfish individual. He was complacent with what he had. No ambitions to better himself. I am totally the opposite; I am always striving to succeed and to better myself and my family."

Eloy: Avoiding Self Hatred "I see my father as any other dude. That has one thing that has motivated me to be so career driven, family oriented and all about success, because I don't want to be just any other dude. I don't want to be like him."

Steve: Avoiding Self Hatred "I am so glad in life that I don't look like him. I would have resented myself if I did look like him. The resentment comes from him not being around and not being a father."

Theme Nineteen: Parenting: The Importance of Paternal Modeling

Jonathan: "Yes, I would like to just find out information about him. How old is he, is he married, does he live? It wouldn't be any anger or frustration. I am past the angry point you could basically say. The angry point was at the beginning when I was a child. When he would keep disappointing me and never show up. I wasn't in my teens more like when I was 10 years old. I want to be a good parent, I want to be the best parent I can be. I want my kids to say to their friends he understands, he never gets angry. I want them to see me as a good parent."

Willy: "No. I wasn't made to be a parent…. I was out of my son's life for the first two years of his life. But I think I am an amazing father. I want to be the type of parent that my son tells people that his father was and always be the reason that I strived for success."

Robert: "I feel like I am a good father, but I could be better. But I think I don't want to do shit like my father did…I am pissed at him but I use it as like…shit I cant do that to my son."

Researcher: "So would you say you being pissed at him has made you a better father?"

Robert: "Yea, I think so. But not…you know…I love my dad but I have a lot of anger towards him for him doing what he did. And me thinking about that shit, I would never want my son to go through that. I would never do that to my son."

Steve: "A good father is one that can sit with you and talk to you about anything. He can open up to you and say what is going on? A father teaches their child and shows interest in their child. A bad father is one who doesn't pay attention to their kids, to their emotions and their needs. If you are not opening yourself to your kids and being open for them, you are not being a father, you are just being a body that's there."

Ruben:  "A good father is one who is continuously trying to improve himself and his children and his family. A good father shows his kids how to be a good human being. A bad father is one who does not spend time with his family."

Researcher:  "Can you describe your idea of a father, in general?"

Ravon  Importance of Paternal Modeling: "Honestly, I can't even answer that question. I don't know what a father is. I guess an absent father is a bad father. Honestly I can't even describe what a good or bad father is because any of the people I have ever hung around with; none of them had close fathers. It was a big group of people without fathers...I wouldn't mind being a parent but I am sure it would take some kind of practice...I think I would make a decent parent. I would learn from my father's mistakes and not make the same ones with my kids. Honestly I have no idea what makes a great parent. Like I would want someone to rate me on my parenting because I don't know what it is. And the Same thing applies to a bad parent. I can't even tell you what a bad parent is, it is like a huge part of what I should have been taught about being a man and a father from my dad is missing."

Mike:  Importance of Paternal Modeling "I don't know what a good father is, from what I have seen so far, basically is someone who is there...someone who tries to do right by their kids. Overall, a good dad is someone who was there who had your back. I really don't know but I guess a bad father is someone who is there but who makes the choice not to be there. Someone who can be there for their kid but actively chooses not to, that is a bad father to me. But yea, I want to be a parent. I think I will be a good dad. I think I will be very involved but somewhat reserved. I will let me kid to figure out their own personality, their likes and dislikes."

Paul: "Yes I want to be a parent and I think I will be a great parent. I think it is evident in my past and my ability to form close relationships… I think a good father is responsible, caring a provider. A bad father is the opposite, someone who doesn't provide and who is not caring. Once you have a child, it is no longer about you, it is all about the child."

Theme Twenty: What makes a Family

Jonathan: "My family is close, we have always been close all of our lives, we always lived together, me my brothers and all my     sisters we moved 5 times in our whole life. We have basically always been together. We still talk at least once or twice a week."

Steve: "My mother is outgoing. She is friendly and like my mom and sister. My older brother is kept to himself and quiet. Younger brother is different He doesn't communicate but he listens and understands. I have step sisters but I don't talk to them. I consider my best friend to be family. I have his mom and his dad. I have my goddaughter's father. We have grown close."

Ruben: "My immediate family is a combination of craziness and fun. My extended family, they are good. I have a supportive family. My brother is sometimes nonexistent when it comes to helping with my mom, but hey, it is what it is."

Ravon: "I have a dysfunctional family. Besides my immediate family, my mother and my grandmother are considered my family."

Mike:       "Family are people who care for my wellbeing and I care for theirs. My family is
            my mom. It is just her and I growing up. I was raised by my grandmother and 4
            aunts. I was raised by all women. My family is my mom. Family are people
            who care for my wellbeing and I care for theirs."

Paul:       "I have a mother and two younger brothers. My mother is a hard working
            mother…I have two younger brothers who both have children. I consider friends
            and blood to be family."

Eloy:       "I only know my mom's side of the family. Were close but we are not super
            close. But I consider family whoever you have a close strong relationship too. It
            could be family but it also could be friends."

Theme Twenty-One: Father's Day

Ruben:      "I miss him during Father's Day. I get emotional thinking that there is a potential
            to fail my son. So I start to become worried. I think as long as my son does not
            have the void that I felt towards my father, and then I feel I would be successful
            as a father. I want my son to recognize that I was there for me."

Steve:      "When Father's Day comes around I always look for a father who I can go
            celebrate with. I am going to enjoy myself and not be miserable. He probably
            doesn't think about me, so why should I think about him."

Ravon:      "On Father's Day I don't even think about my father; for what?"

Mike:       "I usually do something with my mom on Father's Day. I get her double gifts
            because she was like mom and dad rolled into one."

Paul:       "I thought about my father on father's day and wanted to visit him at the cemetery
            but I did not go. On Father's Day I want to spotlight my brothers who are fathers

now. I celebrate them because they are fathers; instead of festering in thoughts of my dad."

Eloy:       "Father's Day is usually treated as "Single Mother's Day" for me."

Theme Twenty-Two: Understanding the Male Role

Jonathan:   "A man is someone who has a lot of responsibilities and takes care of those responsibilities. A man who is there for people. My father did not fit that role as a man when I was ten but now maybe he does. I am starting to ease into that role as a man."

Willy:      "A man can only be judged by the solidity of his word…a person who does not stand by their word and breaks their promises is a coward. A man works for his family. If I make a promise to my son I will go through hell to keep it."

Robert:     "I know I am a man bro, but sometimes I feel like a kid still. And I trip out too because, I feel like I didn't….I don't want to use it as an excuse but I feel I was grown so quick. I mean fuck, I didn't have time to be a kid."

Steve:      "When do you become a man, is it when you first have sex, when you make your first dollar, no! You have to grow into a man and become a man. Being a man you have to own up to your own responsibilities. No one can make you into a man, you have to earn it for yourself... A man is someone who owns up to their responsibilities."

Ruben:      "A man is a provider and protector."

Ravon:      "All the men in my life were not really men, at least I wouldn't consider them that. My idea of a man is kind of blank."

Mike:     "A man is somebody who deals with his shit. Men handle their problems head on. If I had to describe it in one word, I would say a man is accountable."

Paul:     "A man is someone who works hard and takes care of business. No bull shit and faces obstacles head on. An example of this is one day when my father physically protected me. I remember as a kid I was 8 or 9 years old walking into a pet store. Some guy was walking out and just threw the door and it hit me. My dad told the guy that he needs to be careful and the man said, "No your son needs to be careful." So my dad beat his ass. I'm glad that he protected me. I feel like that is a good example of a man."

Eloy:     "A man is somebody who handles all of their business; someone who understands their responsibilities."

www.ingramcontent.com/pod-product-compliance
Lightning Source LLC
Chambersburg PA
CBHW060621290526
45793CB00001B/102